PURSUING

HIS

I CAN
BLESS
THE
LORD!

PRESENCE

DAILY PRAYER. AND FORGIVE (OUR) MY SINS AS WE I HAVE
FORGIVEN Those That have SINNED Against (US) ME
MAT 6:12
make an appt c God daily (Quiet space)

PURSUING HIS PRESENCE

DAVID CERULLO

WHITAKER
HOUSE

PURSUING HIS PRESENCE:
Intimacy with God Revealed in the Tabernacle

David Cerullo
Inspiration Ministries
P.O. Box 7750
Charlotte, NC 28241
www.inspiration.org

ISBN: 978-1-60374-893-3
eBook ISBN: 978-1-60374-894-0
Printed in the United States of America
© 2013 by David Cerullo

Whitaker House
1030 Hunt Valley Circle
New Kensington, PA 15068
www.whitakerhouse.com

Library of Congress Cataloging-in-Publication Data (Pending)

1 2 3 4 5 6 7 8 9 10 11 WU 19 18 17 16 15 14 13

DEDICATION

This book is lovingly dedicated to all those who are seeking a deeper, more intimate relationship with God, those who truly want an encounter with Him that will take them beyond head knowledge and into an experience of intimacy, power, and transformation.

CONTENTS

INTRODUCTION:

AN INVITATION TO INTIMACY

We're about to embark together on an incredible journey—one I'm convinced will transform your life and bring you to a level of relationship, intimacy, and power with God as you've never experienced before. Something special and unique awaits you as you journey through the pages of this book with me.

The fact that you have picked up this book and begun to read it is evidence God has something special for you in mind. Your heavenly Father has scheduled this time—made this appointment with you—to reveal hidden mysteries in the pictures and patterns of His Word that will bring you to a special place where He's been waiting for you.

As we walk this path together, please consider me both a fellow student of the Word and a guide for this journey. I'm not the teacher. I certainly don't have all the answers, nor do I fully understand all the hidden mysteries of Scripture, but I've uncovered some amazing revelations that I'm going to share with you.

In my personal journey with God, I've learned there are mysteries and revelations hidden in His Word—mysteries He's placed there for you and me to search out. There are patterns and pictures within His Word, not just words on paper but pictures He wants us to see.

The Bible says, *"It is the glory of God to conceal a matter, but the glory of kings is to search out a matter"* (Proverbs 25:2 NKJV). True riches and treasure aren't found lying around on the ground in plain sight. Whether you're searching for silver, gold, or precious stones, you have to dig for them, mine for them, and search for them. So, we're about to embark on a treasure hunt—an expedition in which we will approach the Bible differently, looking for pictures and following patterns in order to find a revelation of the mysteries God has hidden in His Word.

One thing is certain: The mysteries and revelations of God's Word are inexhaustible. The more I learn, or the more I think I know, the more I discover that I don't know. There's always more to learn. I'm reminded of the remark from John 21:25: *"And there are also many other things which Jesus did, which if they were written in detail, I suppose that even the world itself would not contain the books that would be written."* The journey we're about to take is like that. It's inexhaustible.

The Power in Five Words

Many years ago, I was reading in Philippians when a specific Scripture passage set me on a journey that changed my life—and continues to do so today. The passage I'm talking about appears in the third chapter of Philippians, in which the apostle Paul expressed his passionate desire to know God more. (See Philippians 3:7–11.) God dropped five words into my spirit that day, and I will introduce those words in detail in chapter 1.

As I began to "search out the matter," the Holy Spirit led me to an unusual Scripture in Ezekiel that seemed to jump off the page at me. Maybe that has happened to you—you're reading the Scriptures when, all of a sudden, a particular word, verse, or passage grabs your attention in a way it never has before.

For me, that Scripture was Ezekiel 43:10–11:

Thou son of man, show the house to the house of Israel, that they may be ashamed of their iniquities: and let them measure the pattern. And if they be ashamed of all that they have done, show them the form of the house...and

*write it in their sight, that they may keep the whole form thereof, and all the
ordinances thereof, and do them.* (KJV)

God was saying to Ezekiel, in effect, "Show My house (the temple) to the
house of Israel (My people). Describe it to them; help them to understand everything about it and its meaning; and help them to see how far they've wandered
from My pattern."

Patterns are important. Imagine trying to make a garment from a piece of
cloth. Unless you have a pattern to place on top of the cloth, chances are, you
won't make the garment to the right dimensions, and it will be unwearable.

With those words from Ezekiel 43, I started on a journey that has taken
me to places with the Lord I never thought imaginable. I began studying the
tabernacle before diving into a study of the temple. I'm still learning and uncov-
ering hidden mysteries along the way, and although there is no way to share in
a single book everything I've learned so far, I will tell you this: Every part of the
tabernacle had purpose, meaning, stories to tell, and mysteries to reveal. In every
component are historical, prophetical, and practical keys from which to draw
personal applications even today.

For example, hidden in the pattern, pictures, and mysteries of the tabernacle
and the temple are prophetic revelations of the duration of the "age of the law"—
the period of time beginning when God gave Moses the Ten Commandments on
top of Mount Sinai and ending with the advent of the Messiah. The patterns of
both the tabernacle and the temple describe the duration of the "age of grace"—
the time period between the end of the Law (and the beginning of grace) until
that day when the Father will send His Son back to earth to rapture the church.
Within the patterns of the tabernacle and the temple, there's even a picture of the
millennial reign of Christ on this earth!

For right now, we're going to take a journey together on a pathway to discover
practical and experiential truths and mysteries hidden within the pictures and
patterns of the tabernacle, the priestly duties, and the furniture itself. I believe
the revelations of the mysteries of the tabernacle are some of the greatest revelations of God, of His Son, of the pathway to His very presence, and of the life-
changing, transforming relationship we can enjoy with Him.

Let's get started!

An Invitation to Intimacy

I'm sure you've looked up into the night sky more than once and wondered about the incredible universe God has created. I often do. Whenever I gaze up at the stars, Psalm 144:3 comes to mind: *"O LORD, what is man, that You take knowledge of him? Or the son of man, that You think of him?"*

I find astronomy fascinating. With all of our science and technology, man hasn't been able to measure the extent of the cosmos. Astronomers speculate that there are literally billions of galaxies. David wrote in Psalm 19:1, *"The heavens are telling of the glory of God; and their expanse is declaring the work of His hands."* That's one thing most scientists and astronomers agree on: The universe is expanding, just as God's Word says it is.

I don't know if you've ever taken a look at the size of our planet Earth in comparison to some of the other planets in our solar system. (See Reference figures D, E, F, and G.) While Earth is larger than Mercury, Venus, Mars, and Pluto, we are dwarfed in comparison to Jupiter, Saturn, Uranus, and Neptune. Jupiter, the largest planet in our solar system, is dwarfed compared to our sun. (See Reference figures H, I, J, and K.) And our sun is dwarfed in comparison to the star Arcturus, which is itself dwarfed by the star Betelgeuse. And on, and on, and on....

My point is that, in all of God's magnificent creation, in the entire expanse of the universe, here is planet Earth, where God made man. And in the midst of all of it, that same God of the universe wants to have a personal, intimate relationship with you and me. It's incredible. Amazing. Unbelievable.

What is man that God is mindful of us? (See Psalm 8:4.)

God created you and me for fellowship and relationship. The garden of Eden was a place where God Himself would walk and talk with Adam and Eve. God gave them dominion over the earth and told them to be fruitful and to multiply. (See Genesis 9:7.) Earth was created to be their dwelling place, and the garden of Eden was where God came to "dwell" with man.

Years later, God would speak to Moses, saying, *"Let [My people] construct a sanctuary for Me, that I may dwell among them"* (Exodus 25:8). The purpose of the tabernacle was to be a dwelling place for God on the earth.

This incredible, amazing, indescribable God wants to dwell—to "tabernacle"—with *you*. That's why it's so important to understand the tabernacle. Hidden within it are pictures, patterns, and mysteries—revelations of how we are to approach His presence.

In the Tabernacle

When King David was just a shepherd boy tending his father's sheep, no doubt he looked up into the same night skies that hold Jupiter, Arcturus, and Betelgeuse, and, in awe, wonderment, and amazement, communed and fellowshipped with God. God referred to him as *"a man after His own heart"* (1 Samuel 13:14). During those months and years spent in solitude in the fields, young David developed a relationship with the Lord characterized by worship and intimacy.

Years later, after he had been made king over Israel, David brought the ark of the covenant to Jerusalem and established the city as the center of worship for the Most High God. Because the temple had not yet been built, David set up a temporary tabernacle to house the ark and appointed priests to minister there before the Lord.

Imagine how overcome with emotion David must have been when the prophet Nathan declared that God was going to establish His kingdom through David's lineage *forever*. After David heard this prophecy, Scripture says that he immediately *"went in and sat before the Lord"* (1 Chronicles 17:16) and poured out his heart to God.

Where did David go to sit before the Lord? The *tabernacle*. Overcome by a sense of worship, humility, and awe at God's goodness and mercy, David wanted to draw as close to Him as possible.

As the sunlight shone through the walls of the tent, it would have cast a shadow over the ark of the covenant. I can just see David crawling into the shadow of the cherubims' wings, desperately trying to draw as close as he could to the presence of the Lord without touching the ark. The cry of his heart was this: *"Hide me in the shadow of Your wings"* (Psalm 17:8).

Like King David, you and I were created to live in intimacy with God. He desires to have an intensely personal relationship with each of us. But what, exactly, does it mean to have an intimate relationship with Him?

We can say that we truly know someone, and are truly known by someone, only when we know each other's deepest thoughts, emotions, and responses; when feelings of closeness, calm, and comfort characterize the relationship. And that is just what it is like to have an intimate relationship with the Lord.

The word *intimate* comes from the Latin word *intimus*, meaning "a close friend." The verb is *intimare*, which means "to make known." To be intimate with someone means to be a close friend, one who is willing to risk making himself or herself known by being open and vulnerable.

God wants us to love and trust Him so much that we invite Him to see into the deepest parts of our lives and hearts, even those parts we try to hide from Him due to fear and shame. He wants us to share ourselves fully with Him and receive His love, just as He desires to share Himself fully with us and receive our love.

I love the picture of intimacy painted for us in the old hymn "In the Garden":

> I come to the garden alone,
> While the dew is still on the roses,
> And the voice I hear, falling on my ear,
> The Son of God discloses.
> And He walks with me, and He talks with me,
> And He tells me I am His own;
> And the joy we share as we tarry there,
> None other has ever known.[1]

In recent years, God has shown me how an intimate relationship with Him enables the believer to live a powerful, peace-filled, overcoming life while having a greater impact in the world for Jesus Christ and His kingdom. Our hunger for Him will take us into the rich places of God, where *"deep calls to deep"* (Psalm 42:7).

When the day finally comes for me to meet Jesus face-to-face, I don't want to merely hear Him say, *"Well done, good and faithful servant"* (Matthew 25:23 KJV, NKJV); I want to be able to run into His outstretched arms and hear Him whisper, "I love you, and I know you love Me. Welcome home." This is the kind of intimate relationship the Lord desires to have with *you*.

---

1. C. Austin Miles, "In the Garden," 1912.

My prayer is that this book will serve as a treasure map to help you discover the pathway leading to a relationship of ever-deepening intimacy with God. I invite you now to journey with me on this pathway leading to His heart.

I will open my mouth in parables, I will utter hidden things, things from of old. —Psalm 78:2 (NIV)

—David Cerullo

10/2/15

PART I

THE PATHWAY TO HIS PRESENCE

1

MISSING THE MARK

"You are in Christ Jesus, who became to us wisdom from God, and righteousness and sanctification, and redemption."
—1 Corinthians 1:30

Whether we realize it or not, every one of us is crying out for more of God's presence. Something inside us yearns to know Him, to experience intimacy with Him, and to offer Him the only thing we have to give—our worship.

My own journey into a relationship of intimacy with the Lord began many years ago with a growing cry in my heart. I was sitting in a hotel room, reading my Bible, in preparation for the message I was to deliver at a conference that evening. I came across this verse written by the apostle Paul: *"that I may know Him and the power of His resurrection"* (Philippians 3:10).

I was blown away when I read those words. I thought, *Paul, how could you possibly say this? You wrote two-thirds of the New Testament, and you're talking about "wanting" to know God? If you felt as though you didn't know God, who else can possibly know Him?*

Then the realization dawned on me that all of us are on a journey into the heart of God, and that none of us will arrive at the end of this pilgrimage until we're in heaven. None of us has reached the place of intimacy with God that He desires us to achieve. Paul was simply saying that he recognized he wasn't yet where God was calling him to be in his relationship with Him, but that he was pressing upward, toward the call of God in Christ Jesus.

I was desperately hungry to know God like this, and so I prayed, "Lord, I want to know You. I don't just want to know *about* You; I want to *know* You."

The Lord then spoke to my spirit, saying, *David, do you want to go to that next level with Me—beyond acquaintance, beyond friendship, beyond knowing about Me? Are you truly longing for a deeper level of relationship?*

I responded, "Yes, Lord, I truly want an intimate relationship with You."

He replied, *David, if you really want to get to know Me, why aren't you spending more time with Me?*

Now, let me be honest with you. When God asked me this, it hurt—a lot. I had been spending time with the Lord, but He was gently and firmly convicting me that I usually limited my time with Him because of my overcrowded schedule.

He went on, *We don't talk very much. You don't spend much time in My presence. If you truly want to know Me, you're going to need to spend more time with Me.*

I thought about this for a while. There are a lot of ways we can get to know someone. Often, when we meet someone for the first time, we've already heard about that person; we just don't really *know* him or her. The only way we get to know others is by spending time with them.

All of us have different kinds of relationships on different levels with different people.

- There are people we've heard about but will never know.

- There are people we've met but will never really get to know, because we don't invest in our relationship by spending time with them.

- There are people we spend more time with and get to know a little bit.

- And then there are those with whom we spend a lot of time, those who eventually become our closest, most intimate friends.

The more time we invest in our relationship with someone, the more we know that person, and the closer we become. This is why the first thing the Lord said to

I don't have a close friend. Ricky must be my friend — intimate — Jenny

me when I prayed for a more intimate relationship with Him was, *If you want to truly know Me, spend time with Me.*

And so I did.

Later that morning, I went down to the hotel restaurant to get some breakfast. As I was sitting there drinking my coffee and considering what God had said about how I needed to spend more time with Him, I sensed He was about to speak to my spirit again. I fished inside my pocket for an envelope and a pen, to write down whatever He was about to tell me.

David, if you truly want to know Me, there are some steps you're going to have to take in order to move into a deeper level of relationship with Me.

"Yes, Lord," I said, "I'll take these steps. Whatever they are, I'll take them." And I quickly scrawled on the envelope the five words the Lord spoke to me:

Repent. Praise. Worship. Offering. Sacrifice.

Little did I know the impact these words would have on my life over the next several years.

Repent

The first step God said I would need to take if I wanted to know Him more intimately was *repent*.

Ouch! That was a tough word for me to hear.

But I understood why He was saying this to me. As believers, we often knock on God's door, wanting to spend time with Him, when we haven't prepared ourselves to enter into His holy presence. The psalmist wrote,

> Who may ascend into the hill of the LORD? And who may stand in His holy place? He who has clean hands and a pure heart, who has not lifted up his soul to falsehood and has not sworn deceitfully. He shall receive a blessing from the LORD and righteousness from the God of his salvation. (Psalm 24:3–5)

When we ask Jesus Christ to be our Lord and Savior, we are immediately washed clean by His blood. Our sins are forgiven, and His righteousness becomes our righteousness: *"You are in Christ Jesus, who became to us wisdom from God, and righteousness and sanctification, and redemption"* (1 Corinthians 1:30).

However, when the disciples asked Jesus to teach them to pray, He told them to pray these words as part of their daily prayer: *"And forgive us our debts* ["sins" TLB], *as we also have forgiven our debtors* ["those who have sinned against us," TLB]" (Matthew 6:12). Although our sin nature is cleansed when we invite Jesus to be the Lord of our lives, we must repent of our sins on a daily basis, as He instructed us to do.

What is sin, exactly? The Greek word for *sin* is *hamartia*, which means "to miss the mark." Sin is anything we do, or fail to do, that causes us to "miss the mark" of God's standard of holiness. We all "miss the mark" repeatedly throughout the day!

This is why Jesus taught us to ask God daily to forgive our sins. Thoughts that shouldn't have been entertained, words that shouldn't have been spoken, actions we should or should not have taken—all these failings occur in our lives on a daily basis. If we are to have *"clean hands and a pure heart,"* which is a qualification for spending time in intimate communion with the Lord, we must repent daily of our sins.

The word repent comes from the Greek word *metaneo*, and it means "to think differently." True repentance requires changing your mind about your sin, and then changing your thinking and your behavior. Refusing or avoiding repentance actually prevents us from having an intimate relationship with the Lord.

Psalm 66:18 reminds us, *"If I regard wickedness in my heart, the Lord will not hear,"* and Isaiah 59:2 sobers us with this warning: *"But your iniquities have made a separation between you and your God, and your sins have hidden His face from you so that He does not hear."*

Now, please understand, I'm *not* saying that God requires us to be perfect. He doesn't. He knows we're weak and vulnerable to temptation. What I *am* saying is that God has provided us with an escape from His judgment for our sin: repentance based on faith in Jesus Christ alone, initially, when we're forgiven for our sin nature, once and for all, and then for the sins we daily commit that can block us from knowing Him more intimately.

Genuine repentance before God is a sign of our brokenness and our desperation for Him. A good example of a prayer of repentance is found in Psalm 51:

> *Be gracious to me, O God, according to Your lovingkindness; according to the greatness of Your compassion blot out my transgressions. Wash me thoroughly*

from my iniquity and cleanse me from my sin....The sacrifices of God are a broken spirit; a broken and a contrite heart, O God, You will not despise.
(Psalm 51:1–2, 17)

God is so glad when we humble ourselves before Him and repent of our sins. He lovingly forgives us and welcomes us into His presence when we ask for His power to strengthen and help us when we "miss the mark."

One Requirement

I want to pause here for a moment and offer you the opportunity to repent before God and invite Jesus Christ to be your Lord and Savior, if you have never done so.

If you're reading this book, I'm assuming it's because you're hungry for an intimate relationship with God. However, until Jesus is the Lord of your life, you will never be able to experience intimacy with God. Why? Because God is holy, and the only way to come into His presence is to be made holy once and for all by the blood of the One who never sinned—Jesus Christ.

Only by accepting that His death on the cross is the one true way leading to God do we *"have confidence to enter the holy place by the blood of Jesus"* (Hebrews 10:19).

But the good news is that you don't have to wait any longer! You can repent of your sinful nature right now and immediately have the awesome right to an intimate relationship with God, who loves you with an everlasting love that will never fail! All you have to do is...

1. Acknowledge you're a sinner.

All have sinned and fall short of the glory of God. (Romans 3:23)

2. Confess your sins.

If we confess our sins, He is faithful and righteous to forgive us our sins and to cleanse us from all unrighteousness. (1 John 1:9)

3. Repent ("change your mind") regarding your sins.

Let the wicked forsake his way, and the unrighteous man his thoughts; and let him return to the Lord, *and He will have compassion on him; and to our God, for He will abundantly pardon.* (Isaiah 55:7)

4. Believe that Jesus is God's Son, who lived a sinless life yet chose to die a sinner's death on the cross to save you from your sins.

If you confess with your mouth Jesus as Lord, and believe in your heart that God raised Him from the dead, you will be saved; for with the heart a person believes, resulting in righteousness, and with the mouth he confesses, resulting in salvation. (Romans 10:9–10)

5. Pray this simple prayer:

Heavenly Father,

Thank You for Your great love for me. I confess that I am a sinner. I repent of my sins and ask You to forgive me. I believe that Jesus Christ is Your Son, that He died on the cross for me, and that You raised Him from the dead. Please wash me clean with His blood. Thank You for forgiving me and making me Your child.

Jesus, please come into my life right now, live in my heart, and fill me with Your Holy Spirit. Be my Savior and Lord. Set me free from every bondage the devil has held in my life.

Jesus, I pray this in Your powerful name.
Amen.

If you just prayed this prayer, then welcome to the family of God! Right now, the angels in heaven are rejoicing over you (see Luke 15:10), and I'm rejoicing over you, too!

In the following days, weeks, and months, you will sense the Lord drawing you into an increasingly intimate relationship. Talk to Him. Read His Word.

Fellowship with other believers. Spend time with Him every day. He loves you so much and wants to be with you. Keep reading this book to discover powerful treasures that will help you draw closer and closer to Him.

Remember, the daily confession of our sins is a powerful step we can take in our journey toward intimacy with God. As we come before Him, washed and cleansed by Jesus' blood and the mercy of God's forgiveness, we're ready to take the next step that will bring us further into His presence.

Digging Deeper

1. Think about a person with whom you have had a close, loving, intimate relationship. What made this relationship special and different from other relationships in your life?

2. Compared to the relationship you just described, how would you like your relationship with the Lord to be the same or different?

3. Consider the time when your relationship with the Lord first began. How has it changed, strengthened, or weakened since then?

4. Spend some time with the Lord and ask Him to reveal areas of your life where you are "missing the mark." When He reveals any sin, simply repent. Tell Him you have "changed your mind" and that, with His courage, grace, and strength, you also will change your thinking and your behavior.

2

STONES CAN'T PRAISE HIM

"Great is the Lord, and highly to be praised."
—Psalm 145:3

The next step God asked me to take in my journey toward a more intimate relationship with Him was *praise*. Although praise had always been an important aspect of my relationship with the Lord, He was asking me to make this a priority in our time together. I nodded in agreement, realizing that, after repentance, praise is the key unlocking the gateway to God's presence.

Since praising God helps lead us to a place of intimacy, it's important we understand exactly what praise is.

Psalm 100:4 declares, *"Enter His gates with thanksgiving and His courts with praise. Give thanks to Him, bless His name."* The Hebrew word for *"praise"* in this verse is *tehillah*, which means "celebration; lauding someone or something that is worthy." When we praise God, we're celebrating His goodness and declaring truths about His worthiness. We celebrate Him for what He has done, what He is doing, and what He will do. With our praise, we acknowledge His greatness:

Every day I will bless You, and I will praise Your name forever and ever. Great is the LORD, and highly to be praised, and His greatness is unsearchable. One generation shall praise Your works to another, and shall declare Your mighty acts. On the glorious splendor of Your majesty and on Your wonderful works, I will meditate. Men shall speak of the power of Your awesome acts; and I will tell of Your greatness. (Psalm 145:2–6)

Praising God inevitably includes thanksgiving:

Give thanks to the LORD, for He is good, for His lovingkindness is everlasting. Give thanks to the God of gods, for His lovingkindness is everlasting. Give thanks to the Lord of lords, for His lovingkindness is everlasting. To Him who alone does great wonders, for His lovingkindness is everlasting. (Psalm 136:1–4)

Our praise for God is based on His greatness, not on our emotions. We can choose to praise Him, regardless of how we're feeling. When the psalmist was overwhelmed with despair, he commanded his soul to praise God and put hope in Him:

Why are you in despair, O my soul? And why are you disturbed within me? Hope in God, for I shall again praise Him, the help of my countenance and my God. (Psalm 43:5)

Why Do We Praise God?

Some might ask, "Well, why should I praise God?" That's a great question, and it's one clearly answered in Scripture. Our praise for God...

+ Declares His worthiness! (See Psalms 48:1; 145:3; Revelation 4:11; 5:12.)

+ Demonstrates our obedience! (See Psalms 150:1; 81:1–4.)

+ Defeats our enemies! (See Psalms 8:1–2; 18:1–3, 46–49.)

+ Delivers us from afflictions! (See Psalms 34:4–8, 108:5–6.)

+ Defies our circumstances! (See Psalm 116.)

We don't praise God because of His need; we praise Him because of our need. When we praise Him, we're acknowledging that there is only one true God and that He is the Lord over our lives. This enables us to draw upon His strength for victory in every situation we encounter.

Praise lifts us up out of the troubles of this world and positions us to receive God's presence, peace, power, protection, and provision. When we praise Him, we're affirming our belief that He is in control of all things!

Once we understand why we are to praise God, we need to understand how to praise Him.

How Do We Praise God?

I believe God intends our praise to be dynamic, enthusiastic, and enjoyable! Here are a few scriptural ways for us to praise the Lord:

By Singing

The Bible is filled with examples of song as a form of praise. Psalm 47:6 commands us not once but four times to sing: "**Sing** *praises to God,* **sing** *praises;* **sing** *praises to our King,* **sing** *praises.*" We encourage ourselves and others with songs that praise God.

The apostle Paul also told us to sing: "[Speak] *to one another in psalms and hymns and spiritual songs,* **singing** *and making melody with your heart to the Lord*" (Ephesians 5:19).

You don't have to be an expert vocalist to sing to the Lord. God hears you singing from your heart, not your vocal cords!

By Shouting

There are more than thirty biblical references to the people of God shouting their praises.

> **Shout** *joyfully to the* LORD, *all the earth; break forth and sing for joy and sing praises. Sing praises to the* LORD *with the lyre, with the lyre and the sound of melody. With trumpets and the sound of the horn* **shout** *joyfully before the King, the* LORD.   (Psalm 98:4–6)

If shouting to God sounds odd to you, think of it this way: When you're at a sporting event and your team wins the game, what do you do? You shout to celebrate the victory! God has won a mighty battle for us, and so we can shout with excitement, joy, and victory to Him! Shouting is a joyful, powerful form of praise that both delights God and scares away the enemy.

By Making Music

Music is a universal expression of creativity. I believe God created music primarily as a means of worshipping Him and delighting our souls. Although the enemy has tried to appropriate music to advance his own kingdom, believers around the world continue to use an amazing variety of instruments to praise God.

The focus of Psalm 150 is praise, and it begins with the words, *"Praise the Lord!"* (Psalm 150:1).The chapter then goes on to list a variety of instruments used to exalt Him. If you are a musician, use instruments to praise God. He has given you this gift, and when you play for Him, you glorify Him. As you praise God with your musical instrument, both God and you will be blessed.

By Using Our Hands

One of the best "instruments" I can play is my own two hands. Psalm 47:1 says, *"O clap your hands, all peoples; shout to God with the voice of joy."* Applause, or hand-clapping, is a powerful and energizing form of praise.

We also can lift our hands toward heaven as an expression of praise: *"Lift up your hands to the sanctuary and praise the Lord"* (Psalm 134:2); *"I will lift up my hands in Your name"* (Psalm 63:4).

The Hebrew word for *hand* is *yah.* The verb form of this is *yadah*, which means "to praise by lifting the hands." Lifting our hands to the Lord is an outward expression of our inward experience of praise.

By Dancing

Dancing before the Lord is an expression of praise that engages every part of us. The Bible says that when the Spirit of the Lord came upon King David, he *"was dancing before the Lord with all his might"* (2 Samuel 6:14).

Just as David's wife Michal despised him for his exuberant expression of praise, there may be some who despise us. But, like David, we can reply, *"I will be more lightly esteemed than this and will be humble in my own eyes"* (2 Samuel 6:22).

Don't Be a Stone!

Keep in mind that praising God isn't something reserved for church services. On the contrary, praise is an attitude, as well as something we choose to do, regardless of our circumstances. When God's praises are continually in our hearts and on our lips, we will be prepared for times of intimacy with Him.

Be aware, however, that although praise helps prepare the way, it's not a guarantee of intimacy with Him. Sadly, many believers who sing loudly, clap enthusiastically, and even dance with all their might before Him, like King David, don't truly know the Lord. This is because intimacy with the Lord involves more than singing songs and declaring truths *about* Him.

In Psalm 148, creation itself is commanded to praise the Lord. However, the stars, sun, and moon don't have a relationship with Him. Jesus said that if His disciples held back their praise, then the stones would have to cry out. (See Luke 19:40.) But stones can't be intimate with the Lord.

Don't be a stone! As you praise the Lord with enthusiasm and joy, know that you can have an intimate relationship with Him. This is His heart's desire. But know, too, that if you truly want to be intimate with the Lord, there are still three more steps to take on the pathway leading to His presence. We will discuss those steps in the next several chapters.

Digging Deeper

1. Since childhood, what has been your experience in praising the Lord?

2. While most of us are probably comfortable with using music, song, and clapping to praise Him, many people are hesitant at the thought of shouting, raising their hands, or dancing. What forms of praise are you comfortable or uncomfortable with? Why? *Comf c all expressions*

3. Are you willing to be bolder in physically expressing your praise to the Lord? Why or why not? *Yes the more I show him that I luv him c my praise the more intimate we will become*

4. Spend time talking to the Lord and praising Him for all He has done, all He is doing, and all He will do in your life and in the lives of your loved ones. Ask Him to give you the courage to boldly praise Him in your quiet time alone with Him and in worship with other believers.

Step 1 Repent

Intimacy/
Repent

Step 2 Praise - when I praise God, I am acknowledging what he does.

Step 3 Worship - I am expressing my love for who He is.

Step 4

Step 5

3

DON'T PUT GOD ON YOUR "TO-DO" LIST

"Come, let us worship and bow down, let us kneel before the
Lord our Maker."
—Psalm 95:6

That morning in the coffee shop, God told me that if I wanted to be intimate with Him, there was a third step I needed to take on the pathway leading into His presence: *David, after you repent and after you praise Me, I want you to* **worship** *Me when you come into My presence.*

I paused to consider exactly what He was saying to me. Some—perhaps even most—of us believe that "praise" and "worship" are synonymous terms for expressing our adoration to God, but I was beginning to understand the inaccuracy of that belief. There is a distinct difference between praise and worship. When I praise God, I am acknowledging what He does, but when I worship Him, I am expressing my love for who He is.

While praise can lead to worship, this progression isn't automatic. The sad truth is that I can praise God without ever experiencing the true intimacy that comes from worshipping Him.

Waiting on the Lord

The Hebrew word used in the Old Testament for *worship* is *shachah*, which means "to stoop, crouch, bow low, fall down flat in an act of submission or reverence before royalty or God." The Greek word for *worship* used predominantly in the New Testament is *proskuneo*, which is a combination of two words: *pros* ("toward") and *kuneo* ("to kiss"). It means "to kiss, like a dog licking its master's hand, to prostrate, bow down, show reverence for, adore."

When I worship the Lord, I submit myself to Him. I bow before Him in absolute humility. I "kiss" Him with my spirit. I honor the One to whom all honor is due.

As I worship the Lord, I commune with Him at the deepest level of my spirit, where "*deep calls to deep*" (Psalm 42:7). In this place of intimacy, I hold nothing back from Him. I invite Him to "into me see." I experience His love for me, and He experiences my love for Him. This is only possible because true worship is a place of absolute trust. I'm not afraid of what God will say or do or expect of me in these moments of vulnerability.

A vital aspect of worship is *waiting* on the Lord. We are told thirty-eight times in the Old Testament to wait on Him. What does this mean?

The Hebrew word for "*wait*" is *yachal*: "to wait, tarry, hope, expect, anticipate."

In Psalm 27:14, David exhorts us, "**Wait** for the Lord; be strong and let your heart take courage; yes, **wait** for the Lord."

The prophet Micah vowed, "*But as for me, I will watch expectantly for the Lord; I will **wait** for the God of my salvation. My God will hear me*" (Micah 7:7).

When we're seeking times of intimacy with God—when we have repented of our sins and praised Him; when we have moved into that place of worship, expressing our love and adoration for Him—it's because we desperately want to experience a sense of His love for us. But the truth is that, because of the limitations of our humanity, we don't always experience His presence and sense Him right there with us.

Waiting as Proof of Our Passion

Many times, God's presence in worship comes only as we wait in hope-filled expectation and anticipation, believing that, as much as we want to be with Him, He wants to be with us even more. Too often, we rush into our quiet times with the Lord, as though He is an item needing to be accomplished and checked off on our "to-do list" after fifteen minutes. We're too content with a mere devotional reading, a verse or two of Scripture, and then a simple prayer in which we express our thanksgiving and praise. We seldom *wait* before the Lord in true worship. God loves it when we linger with Him, and even seems to deliberately pause to make sure we truly desire to be with Him before blessing us with an overwhelming awareness of His presence.

In Acts 1:4, Jesus told His disciples to remain in Jerusalem and *"wait for what the Father had promised."* We also know from 1 Corinthians 15:6 that Jesus had appeared to five hundred of His followers after His resurrection from the dead. Do you know that of these five hundred, only one hundred twenty disciples were in the upper room on the day of Pentecost, fellowshipping together, praying, and waiting on the Lord? Only one hundred twenty tarried. Only one hundred twenty were changed because they waited. Only one hundred twenty experienced a powerful outpouring of His presence—a mere 24 percent.

The other three hundred eighty followers chose to do something else that day, and by making that choice, they missed out on an indescribable blessing. Wouldn't it have been terrible to be one of the disciples who got tired of waiting and just went on home because they were busy or bored?

Waiting in the Midst of Suffering

Sometimes, we may feel as though it's simply too hard to wait on the Lord, especially when we're in the midst of painful circumstances. We may grow impatient with God, believing that if He only knew how much we were suffering, He wouldn't make us wait for His presence to come and comfort us.

But the reality is that God's presence doesn't manifest in response to our suffering; it comes in response to our brokenness. When we're broken, the heavens open.

The righteous cry, and the LORD hears and delivers them out of all their troubles. The LORD is near to the brokenhearted, and saves those who are crushed in spirit. Many are the afflictions of the righteous, but the LORD delivers him out of them all. (Psalm 34:17–19)

As we wait on the Lord day by day, in worshipful, hope-filled expectation, He comes and ministers His comfort, strength, healing, and hope to us. Never underestimate the power of time spent in God's presence. In a single moment, we can be healed and our circumstances changed. Jacob had an encounter in God's presence (see Genesis 32:24–32), and in a moment…

+ His name was changed.

+ His walk was changed.

+ His entire destiny was changed!

There's a wonderful chorus I love to sing called "In the Presence of Jehovah," by Geron and Becky Davis:

> In the presence of Jehovah
> God Almighty, Prince of Peace
> Troubles vanish, hearts are mended
> In the presence of the King.

My friend, there are things you simply can't find in the Lord's presence: sin, sickness, doubt, worry, guilt, fear, depression, loneliness, and heartache. All of these must disappear when confronted with God's power and love. As you faithfully wait on Him in worship, you will discover that *anything* can happen in the presence of the King!

Does spending time with God sometimes feel like a burden, a religious obligation, or a chore? If so, cross off His name from your "to-do" list forever! Be willing to *wait* on Him, trusting that He simply wants to *be* with you and bless you with His amazing love.

I invite you to enter into the intimacy of true worship before the Lord. I promise that you won't regret taking this vital, life-changing step on your journey into the heart of God.

Digging Deeper

1. The primary difference between praise and worship is that when we praise God, we're acknowledging *what He does*, and when we worship Him, we're expressing our love for *who He is*. Describe the difference between praise and worship as you have experienced them in your life.

2. Is it easy or difficult for you to openly express your love for the Lord? Why? *Easy because I realize that he loves me he has loved me all my life. I'm learning to trust him.*

3. The original Greek word meaning *worship* that's used in the New Testament means "to kiss, like a dog licking its master's hand, to prostrate, bow down, show reverence for, adore." Are you comfortable with this definition? Why or why not? *Yes because He's the Supreme being I would not exist without him*

4. Spend time with the Lord in worship. As you humble yourself before Him and express your love, be willing to wait on Him, knowing that anything can happen in God's presence.

4

HE WANTS IT ALL

"And my God will supply all your needs according to His riches in glory in
Christ Jesus."
—Philippians 4:19

As I sat sipping my coffee and pondering what the Lord was saying to me about repentance, praise, and worship, He gave me yet another step to take on the pathway into His presence: *offering.*

He said, *David, after you have repented, after you have praised Me, after you have entered into true worship, know that My requirements for intimacy also include bringing me an* **offering.**

Since my wife, Barbara, and I have always tithed faithfully, when God told me that bringing Him an offering was one of the five steps to intimacy with Him, I paid attention. I realized He was talking about more than giving Him 10 percent of my weekly paycheck.

When church folks hear the word *offering,* they usually begin looking around for the ushers and the offering plate. To be sure, faithfully giving financial gifts to the Lord is a vital step on one's journey toward intimacy with Him. Why?

Because our level of giving reflects our level of trust in God and our belief in His desire and ability to provide for our every need. When we give Him our tithes and special offerings, we're demonstrating our trust in His promise to abundantly bless our obedience and rebuke the devourer for our sake.

> *"Bring the whole tithe into the storehouse, so that there may be food in My house, and test Me now in this," says the* Lord *of hosts, "if I will not open for you the windows of heaven, and pour out for you a blessing until it overflows. Then I will rebuke the devourer for you, so that it may not destroy the fruits of the ground; nor will your vine in the field cast its grapes," says the* Lord *of hosts. "And all the nations will call you blessed, for you shall be a delightful land," says the* Lord *of hosts.* (Malachi 3:10–12)

So, yes, consistently giving back to God a portion of what He has given to us is vital to experiencing intimacy with Him. But when He told me that I needed to bring Him an offering in my intimate times with Him, I knew He was requiring more of me than my wallet. You see, *nothing* I have is "mine."

Mine!

As the parents of two children and the grandparents of five, Barbara and I are well acquainted with a two-year-old's tendency to grab a favorite toy and clutch it tightly, while loudly declaring, "Mine!" Any attempts to remove the coveted object typically result in loud objections accompanied by dramatic sobs.

Many believers act the same. Somewhere along the way, we got the mistaken notion that whatever is within our grasp belongs to us. My friend, this simply isn't so. Everything we own is in our possession *only* because God has given it to us or allowed us to have it. *Nothing* belongs to us, as King David declared:

> **Yours**, O Lord, *is the greatness and the power and the glory and the victory and the majesty, indeed everything that is in the heavens and the earth;* **Yours** *is the dominion, O* Lord, *and You exalt Yourself as head over all. Both riches and honor come from You, and You rule over all, and in* **Your** *hand is power and might; and it lies in* **Your** *hand to make great and to strengthen everyone.* (1 Chronicles 29:11–12)

This means that every material belonging—clothes, cars, furniture, houses, books computers, checkbooks, credit cards—it *all* belongs to God. Although we may cry out, "Mine!" when something we think we own is threatened, the truth is, it's *His*! The Lord calls us to love Him more than all our worldly goods.

The same is true of our time and talents—neither belongs to us. As with our treasure, our time, skills, and spiritual gifts are God's, to be used at His discretion. When we are moving into intimacy with Him, we will clearly hear Him tell us when and where and how to use these resources that He has so lovingly and generously given us.

It's easy to be afraid that if we let go of the little bit of treasure, time, or talents we have, there won't be enough left over for us. But this simply isn't true. In God's economy, when we let go of what we have as a demonstration of worship and obedience to Him, He multiplies our offerings back to us in the form of His blessings in our lives.

All!

Many of us are very familiar with this comforting passage from Philippians 4:19: *"And my God will supply* **all** *your needs according to His riches in glory in Christ Jesus."* But many of us are unfamiliar with the verse that precedes it:

But I have received everything in full and have an abundance; I am amply supplied, having received from Epaphroditus what you have sent, a fragrant aroma, an acceptable sacrifice, well-pleasing to God. (Philippians 4:18)

The relationship between these two verses is pretty subtle, so it can be easy to miss. In Philippians 4:18, Paul tells the folks in the church at Philippi that he has received the sacrificial gift they had sent him, and in the next verse, he tells them that because they supplied his needs, God would supply their needs.

Do you see the correlation? The Philippian believers must have had an intimate, trusting relationship with the Lord, because they were willing to give generously to take care of God's servant. And Paul assured them that this trust was not unfounded, because God would supply *all* their needs. How much is "all"? *All!*

Paul also wrote to the Corinthian church about giving generous offerings and then trusting God to supply all their needs:

Let each one give as he purposes in his heart, not grudgingly or of necessity; for God loves a cheerful giver. And God is able to make all grace abound toward you, that you, always having all sufficiency in all things, may have an abundance for every good work. (2 Corinthians 9:8–9 NKJV)

What did Paul say would happen if the Corinthians cheerfully worshipped God with their offerings? God would make *"all grace abound"* to them, and they would have *"all sufficiency"* in everything they needed. How much is "all"? All!

If we desire intimacy with the Lord, we must acknowledge that *all* we have and *all* we are is His. And if He should require any amount of our time, talent, or treasure, we must willingly relinquish anything and everything to Him and then trust Him to supply *all* our needs.

My friend, don't be afraid to worship the Lord with your offerings. Choose to trust Him with everything you are and everything you have. As you do, you will experience increasingly deeper levels of intimacy with the One who loves you so.

Digging Deeper

1. What has been your life experience with tithing and giving God special offerings? Are you trusting in His promise in Malachi 3:10–12 to bless your giving and rebuke the devourer in response to your faithful giving? Why or why not?

2. Is there anything you are calling "Mine!" and withholding from the Lord?

3. Are you willing now to give God *all* that you have and *all* that you are? Why or why not? Be honest with yourself and with Him.

4. Spend time with the Lord, asking Him to reveal anything you may be clutching to yourself. Agree with Him that, according to 1 Chronicles 29:11–12, everything you have belongs to Him. Ask Him to help you release *all* things into His care and to help you trust Him to supply *all* of your needs because of His great love for you.

5

BURNT FLESH

"I urge you, brethren, by the mercies of God, to present your bodies a living and holy sacrifice, acceptable to God, which is your spiritual service of worship."
—Romans 12:1

The fifth and final word God spoke to me that morning in the hotel coffee shop was *sacrifice*. Now there's a word that could make a person nervous! But because I trust in God's amazing love for me, I knew He wasn't asking anything of me I wasn't able to give Him.

"Lord," I responded, "what do You mean? What kind of sacrifice do You want me to bring You?"

He replied, *David, you can't bring Me an offering without sacrifice.*

I thought of the story in 2 Samuel 24, when King David wanted to build an altar to the Lord; although Araunah freely offered to give him all the items he needed for the sacrifice, he insisted on paying for the supplies, declaring, *"I will not offer burnt offerings to the LORD my God which cost me nothing"* (2 Samuel 24:24).

David knew he needed to pay a price for his offering. He realized his gift required a sacrifice on his part if it was to be meaningful to both him and God.

What was true for King David then is still true for us today. God doesn't want our token offerings that basically cost us nothing—a $10 check in the offering plate when we typically spend $100 on every trip to the mall; serving someone in need only when it's convenient for us; a quick, ten-minute devotional reading squeezed into our morning routine just so we can say we spent time with Him.

God doesn't want our second best, and He isn't interested in mere crumbs from our table. No, God was telling me that morning that if I want to be intimate with Him, then I must be willing to make *sacrifices* for Him. The gifts of my time, talent, and treasure have to cost me something. If our gifts are precious to us, they will be precious to God, as well.

When God asked Abraham if he was willing to sacrifice his son Isaac, He was testing Abraham to see if he was willing to offer Him the most precious thing in the world to him: the promise for which Abraham and Sarah had waited for twenty-seven years. And Abraham demonstrated with his obedience that he was willing:

> *By Myself I have sworn, declares the* Lord, *because you have done this thing and have not withheld your son, your only son, indeed I will greatly bless you, and I will greatly multiply your seed as the stars of the heavens and as the sand which is on the seashore; and your seed shall possess the gate of their enemies. In your seed all the nations of the earth shall be blessed, because you have obeyed My voice.* (Genesis 22:16–18)

Because Abraham withheld nothing but rather offered everything, God blessed him by confirming and then fulfilling the covenant He had made with him years before—and his offspring indeed became *"as the stars in the heavens"* and *"as the sand which is on the seashore"*!

Likewise, I believe the Lord was asking something else of me that morning. I sensed He was asking me if I would be willing to offer my very *life* as a living sacrifice to Him.

Living Sacrifices

You know, the painful truth is that I could...

+ repent every day;

+ praise God with enthusiasm;

+ worship Him passionately;

+ offer Him *all* of my time, treasure, and talent; and

+ give Him the most precious thing in the world to me,

…but there still would be one thing preventing me from walking in a deeply intimate relationship with the Lord: *Me.*

Just like a wife who willingly cooks the meals, cleans the house, and meets all of her husband's physical needs but withholds the deepest part of her heart and soul from him, so we, too, can serve the Lord faithfully without ever being truly intimate with Him.

You see, intimacy with the Lord means giving myself to Him with *abandon.* I may do everything He tells me to do and give Him everything He asks me to give, but if I withhold myself from Him, I will never experience true intimacy with the Lord.

In his letter to the Roman Christians, Paul wrote,

I urge you therefore, brethren, by the mercies of God, to present your bodies a living and holy sacrifice, acceptable to God, which is your spiritual service of worship. And do not be conformed to this world, but be transformed by the renewing of your mind, so that you may prove what the will of God is, that which is good and acceptable and perfect. (Romans 12:1–2)

Most of us think that the word *sacrifice* means "to give up something." In Hebrew, the word *sacrifice* is *korban.* It means "to draw near to." The goal of the tabernacle sacrifices was to draw God's people near to Him. This is what God wants you and me to do.

Many of us spend our lives hopping on and off of God's altar. Our hearts can be stirred with passion, and we may give ourselves to Him as a living sacrifice, drawing near to Him for a day, a week, or a month, but then we find "better" things to do. Like Peter, we vow that we're willing to go with the Lord, even to death. (See Luke 22:33.) But then, when the fire gets too painful or it seems as though God's requirements are too hard, instead of pressing further into Him, we jump off and run away with our flesh only half burnt away. And burnt flesh smells pretty bad!

To continue on this pathway into the intimacy of God's presence, we must choose to climb up on His altar and offer ourselves—body, soul, and spirit—as a living sacrifice; to draw near to Him and allow His bonds of love to hold us in place until every part of our flesh that does not bring Him glory has been consumed.

Then, like Paul, we will be able to say, "*I have been crucified with Christ; and it is no longer I who live, but Christ lives in me; and the life which I now live in the flesh I live by faith in the Son of God, who loved me and gave Himself up for me*" (Galatians 2:20).

The Cry of the Desperate

In Mark 10, we read the story of a blind man named Bartimaeus who was desperate for an encounter with Jesus. Bartimaeus spent his days sitting by the side of the road, begging for food, money—anything that could temporarily alleviate the painful circumstances of his life.

But then, one day, he heard Jesus and His disciples passing by. "*When he heard that it was Jesus the Nazarene, he began to cry out and say, 'Jesus, Son of David, have mercy on me!'*" (Mark 10:47).

It appeared that Jesus was going to just walk on by the blind beggar. In response to those who tried to silence his cries, Bartimaeus simply cried out all the more, "*Son of David, have mercy on me!*" (Mark 10:48).

Bartimaeus knew that one encounter with Jesus could impact his life forever. He was desperate for change, and so he was not ashamed to cry out to Jesus. He persistently refused to be silenced or embarrassed by the opinions of others, and his persistence was honored when Jesus responded to his cries and healed his blindness. (See Mark 10:49–52.)

My friend, are you desperate for an encounter with the Lord? Do you have a hunger for intimacy with Him that cannot be satisfied any other way? Are you willing to take these five steps that will lead you on the pathway to His presence? If so, cry out for His touch as you...

+ repent before Him.

- praise Him wholeheartedly.
- worship Him passionately.
- offer Him your time, treasure, and talents.
- remain a living sacrifice on His altar.

If you are ready to take these five steps, then come with me now as we continue on this journey.

Digging Deeper

1. Think about the offerings you have given to the Lord in recent months. Have they been your second best, or have they truly cost you something?

2. How does it make you feel to know that God is calling you to be a "living sacrifice" for Him?

3. Have you given yourself to the Lord with abandon? Why or why not?

4. Spend time with God now repenting for any sin, praising Him, worshipping Him, and offering Him your all. Ask Him for His courage, grace, and strength to be a living sacrifice for Him, to His glory.

PART II

THE JOURNEY BEGINS

6

THE CHOICE IS YOURS

"Then God said, 'Let Us make man in Our image.'"
—Genesis 1:26

Do we look like God? Does God have the same physical features as we have? Does God look like us? What is the image of God we bear?

I don't believe that being made in God's image has anything to do with our physical features. Instead, God's image is found in our power of *choice*. We've been given the ability to choose—to make our own decisions.

He didn't create us like robots or puppets. He doesn't pull some cosmic string that causes us to worship Him. He sets choices before us throughout our lives. If we love Him, worship Him, praise Him, and seek Him, it's because we choose to, not because there is some kind of mystical unseen hand forcing us to do so. After all, no one wants a forced love affair.

The power to choose is an incredible characteristic God imparted to us.

What if I told you that you could have as much of a relationship with God as you would like? What if you could experience as much of His presence as you wanted? How much of a relationship with God—the Creator of heaven and earth, the Maker of the universe and all it contains—would you like to have? The choice is yours. You can experience as much or as little of God as you choose.

This book is meant to help you discover a pathway to an incredible relationship with God Himself. But you must decide: Will you be satisfied with knowing only *about* the Lord? Do you desire mere acquaintance with Him? Or do you want to move beyond acquaintance to a place of deep intimacy?

An Investment of Time

The Father longs to have an intimate relationship with you. But intimate relationships take time. They take time to develop, and they take time to sustain and grow. You can't possibly have an intimate relationship with someone you see or talk to once a year, once a month, or even once a week. Relationships develop as a result of choosing to spend quality time together.

Before Moses died, and before he turned the leadership of the nation of Israel over to Joshua, he called the people together at a place called Shechem, a city that sat between Mount Ebal and Mount Gerizim. It was also the first place God brought Abraham after promising him the land. Can you imagine what Moses had to say to the children of Israel after leading them for forty years and knowing that soon he would depart? He wanted them to remember his final words, knowing they were about to finally cross the Jordan River and venture into the Promised Land.

Moses told Joshua to choose twelve men, one from each of the tribes of Israel, and to divide them into two companies. Joshua sent six men from the tribes of Simeon, Levi, Judah, Issachar, Joseph, and Benjamin to stand on top of Mount Gerizim, as representatives of God's blessing. To represent God's curse, he sent another six men, from the tribes of Reuben, Gad, Asher, Zebulun, Dan, and Naphtali, to stand on Mount Ebal.

And Moses instructed them what to do next:

The Levites shall then answer and say to all the men of Israel with a loud voice, "Cursed is the man who makes an idol or a molten image, an abomination to the Lord, the work of the hands of the craftsman, and sets it up in secret." And all the people shall answer and say, "Amen." "Cursed is he who dishonors his father or mother." And all the people shall say, "Amen." "Cursed is he who moves his neighbor's boundary mark." And all the people shall say, "Amen." "Cursed is he who misleads a blind person on the road." And all the people shall say, "Amen." "Cursed is he who distorts the justice due an alien, orphan, and widow." And all the people shall say, "Amen." "Cursed is he who lies with his father's wife, because he has uncovered his father's skirt." And all the people shall say, "Amen." "Cursed is he who lies with any animal." And all the people shall say, "Amen." "Cursed is he who lies with his sister, the daughter of his father or of his mother." And all the people shall say, "Amen." "Cursed is he who lies with his mother-in-law." And all the people shall say, "Amen." "Cursed is he who strikes his neighbor in secret." And all the people shall say, "Amen." "Cursed is he who accepts a bribe to strike down an innocent person." And all the people shall say, "Amen." "Cursed is he who does not confirm the words of this law by doing them." And all the people shall say, "Amen." (Deuteronomy 27:14–26)

Those are sobering words, to say the least. What must the people have been thinking? Then Moses told them what would happen as a result:

Now it shall be, if you diligently obey the LORD YOUR GOD, being careful to do all His commandments which I command you today, the LORD your God will set you high above all the nations of the earth. All these blessings will come upon you and overtake you if you obey the LORD your God: "Blessed shall you be in the city, and blessed shall you be in the country. Blessed shall be the offspring of your body and the produce of your ground and the offspring of your beasts, the increase of your herd and the young of your flock. Blessed shall be your basket and your kneading bowl. Blessed shall you be when you come in, and blessed shall you be when you go out. The LORD shall cause your enemies who rise up against you to be defeated before you; they will come out against you one way and will flee before you seven ways. The LORD will command the blessing upon you in your barns and in all that you put your hand to, and He will bless you in the land which the LORD your God gives you. The LORD will establish you as a holy people to Himself, as He swore to you, if you keep the commandments of the LORD your God and walk in His ways. So all the peoples of the earth will see that you are called by the name of the LORD, and they will be afraid of you. The LORD will make you abound in prosperity, in the offspring of your body and in the offspring of your beast and in the produce of your ground, in the land which the LORD *swore to your fathers to give you. The* LORD *will open for you His good storehouse, the heavens, to give rain to your land in its season and to bless all the work of your hand; and you shall lend to many nations, but you shall not borrow. The* LORD *will make you the head and not the tail, and you only will be above, and you will not be underneath, if you listen to the commandments of the* LORD *your God, which I charge you today, to observe them carefully, and do not turn aside from any of the words which I command you today, to the right or to the left, to go after other gods to serve them."* (Deuteronomy 28:1–14)

The blessings for choosing to be obedient to the Lord rang out, followed by a brief moment of silence. The people must have been wondering what was happening. Then Moses warned them what would happen if they ignored God's warnings. (See Deuteronomy 28:15–68.)

It seemed like these curses wouldn't end. The people must have been wondering, *What is this all about?*

Why did God first bring Abraham to this place, and why was He now bringing the children of Israel there? He brought them there for one purpose: To offer them a choice, to be blessed or be cursed. A choice to become either the special, peculiar, called-out people of God, or a people who would suffer the consequences of their disobedient choices.

Mount Gerizim became known as "the mount of blessing," and Mount Ebal as "the mount of cursing." Shechem, the city in between, became "the place of choosing."

Moses would soon leave. Joshua would assume command of Israel and would lead them across the Jordan and into the Promised Land after forty long years of wandering in the wilderness. Israel would face many conquests and battles along the way, beginning with Jericho and moving on to take the northern and southern portions of Palestine. Eventually, Joshua would divide the Promised Land among the tribes of Israel.

Like Moses before him, Joshua was concerned about what would happen to the children of Israel after he was gone. Would they continue to choose to serve and obey the Lord, or would they rebel?

The Place of Choosing

When Joshua called all of Israel together to receive for his final words of instructions, where do you think he convened the meeting? He chose Shechem, the place of choosing.

> Now it came about after many days, when the Lord had given rest to Israel from all their enemies on every side, and Joshua was old, advanced in years, that Joshua called for all Israel, for their elders and their heads and their judges and their officers, and said to them, "I am old, advanced in years. And you have seen all that the Lord your God has done to all these nations because of you, for the Lord your God is He who has been fighting for you. See, I have apportioned to you these nations which remain as an inheritance for your tribes, with all the nations which I have cut off, from the Jordan even to the Great Sea toward the setting of the sun. The Lord your God, He will thrust them out from before you and drive them from before you; and you will possess their land, just as the Lord your God promised you. Be very firm, then, to keep and do all that is written in the book of the law of Moses, so that you may not turn aside from it to the right hand or to the left, so that you will not associate with these nations, these which remain among you, or mention the name of their gods, or make anyone swear by them, or serve them, or bow down to them. But you are to cling to the Lord your God, as you have done to this day. For the Lord has driven out great and strong nations from before you; and as for you, no man has stood before you to this day. One of your men puts to flight a thousand, for the Lord your God is He who fights for you, just as He promised you. So take diligent heed to yourselves to love the Lord your God." (Joshua 23:1–11)

Joshua had been a faithful leader, and now he was about to die. He closed his remarks with a final instruction, which has become familiar to most of us:

> Choose for yourselves this day whom you will serve, whether the gods which your fathers served that were on the other side of the River, or the gods of the Amorites, in whose land you dwell. **But as for me and my house, we will serve the Lord.** (Joshua 24:15 NKJV)

If Israel wanted to experience God's blessing, they had to choose to be obedient, choose to love the Lord, and choose to serve Him with all their hearts.

Every day, you and I face a choice about our relationship with our heavenly Father. We each have our own "Shechem"—our own place of choosing.

What kind of a relationship with your heavenly Father do you want? Do you want to simply know *about* Him? Or do you want to move past the point of mere acquaintance to friendship? Do you want to move past friendship to a place of intimacy?

Relationships happen on many levels. You can know about someone. You can hear about someone. You can be friends with someone. You can even have an intimate relationship with someone. Each requires a different investment of your time into the relationship. The level of your relationship will ultimately depend on how much time you choose to spend with the other person.

There is a level with the Lord that you and I can get to. It is a place of incredible power and intimacy, but it will require a sacrifice of your time. It's a sacrifice I pray you will choose to make, because it will take you to places with God you've never been to before.

Each day, like Joshua, we need to not only say, *"As for me and my house, we will serve the LORD"*; we also need to say, "This day, today, I make a choice to spend time with Him—time in His Word, time in prayer, time in worship—more time with Him."

Each day, we need our daily bread. We can't survive or remain healthy in the natural world if we eat only one meal per month, or even one meal per week. We'd die. The same is true spiritually.

Today, I pray you will make a commitment to spend daily time with the Lord. Time in His Word...time in prayer...time in worship...time alone with Him. He will nourish you on "daily bread" as you bask in His presence.

Get ready to embark on a life-changing path that will draw you straight into the very heart of God. Discover the joy of ever-deepening intimacy with the Lord. Experience His presence in ways you've never known before.

The choice is yours.

Digging Deeper

1. What kind of a relationship with God—the Creator of heaven and earth, the Maker of the universe and all it contains—would you like to have?

2. Are there times in your life when you felt cursed because you had abandoned your relationship with God? How so?

3. List some of the blessings that have followed as you have been obedient to God and His calling. If you can't think of any, could there be a reason?

4. How would you describe your relationship with God right now? Is it one where you simply know *about* Him, one of acquaintance or friendship, or one of deep intimacy?

5. What would it mean for you to take your relationship with God to a higher level?

7

PICTURES, PATTERNS, AND MYSTERIES

"You will seek Me and find Me, when you search for Me with all your heart."
—Jeremiah 29:13

When you were a kid, did you ever pretend to be a pirate and make a map where an "X" marked the spot to treasure buried in your backyard? The Word of God is sort of like a treasure map, except that the treasure contained within isn't pretend; it's pure gold! Just as a treasure map leads to buried riches, when we diligently follow the map of the Bible, we discover the amazing riches He's buried there for us to find. But we must dig for them.

As I have studied the Bible over the years, God has revealed mysteries that have profoundly impacted me on my journey toward intimacy with Him. Now, let me assure you, He hasn't been showing me these secrets because I'm someone special. God has been sharing deep truths with me because I've asked Him, I've pursued Him, and I've waited and listened for His answers. My friend, He wants to share His mysteries with you, too.

King Solomon observed, *"It is the glory of God to conceal a matter, but the glory of kings is to search out a matter"* (Proverbs 25:2). Most times, the deep things of God are not clearly understood by our natural minds. He begins to reveal the hidden treasures of His Word only as we passionately search for Him, driven by a desperate hunger to truly know Him and His ways. When we dig for God's gold buried within Scripture, He assures us, *"You will seek Me and find Me, when you search for Me with all your heart"* (Jeremiah 29:13).

As I sought God and asked Him to reveal Himself to me through His Word, He reminded me of His promise in James 4:8: *"Draw near to God and He will draw near to you."* And so, I began to draw near to Him in ways I never had before; and, as I did, He started revealing to me the pictures and patterns hidden in His Word.

Painted Pictures

When I was a little boy, my parents were faithful in taking me to Sunday school. I loved the big Bible in the children's department at our church because it was full of pictures. I would turn the pages slowly, captivated by the illustrations of Noah and the ark, Moses parting the Red Sea, and Daniel in the lions' den.

The Bible is full of pictures. But, as adults, we tend to read the words printed on the pages without seeing the amazing pictures God has painted for us in His Word.

He has included these pictures because He is trying to teach us a vital truth about how He communicates with His children: God uses the *natural* world to reveal deep *spiritual* truths to us.

Jesus frequently used the natural to reveal the spiritual by teaching His followers in parables—earthly stories with heavenly meanings. He revealed truths about God's kingdom through a seed, a pearl, and a fishnet. (See Matthew 13:31–32, 45–48; Mark 4:26–32; Luke 13:18–19.) He used a flock of sheep and a shepherd to teach how His disciples are to follow Him and listen for His voice. (See John 10:1–18.) He pointed to a grapevine and its branches to demonstrate our need to abide in Him if we want to bear good fruit for eternity. (See John 15:1–8.)

When the disciples came to Jesus and asked why He taught in parables, He replied, *"To you it has been granted to know the mysteries of the kingdom of heaven, but to them it has not been granted"* (Matthew 13:11).

The mysteries of heaven are like treasures of gold imbedded deep in God's Word that must be mined if they are to be discovered, understood, and applied to our lives.

The Natural and the Spiritual

In his letter to the Roman Christians, Paul said, *"For the invisible things of him from the creation of the world are clearly seen, being understood by the things that are made, even his eternal power and Godhead; so that they are without excuse"* (Romans 1:20 KJV).

Paul was saying that God has used what is visible to teach about what is invisible. He emphasized the same point in his letter to the believers in Corinth: *"So also it is written, 'The first* MAN, *Adam,* BECAME A LIVING SOUL.' *The last Adam became a life-giving spirit.* **However, the spiritual is not first, but the natural; then the spiritual"** (1 Corinthians 15:45–46).

Let me say it again: God uses the natural to reveal the spiritual. He uses pictures and patterns from the temporal world to teach us eternal truths.

When I cried out to God in my hunger to know Him more intimately, I was amazed as He began revealing to me the mysteries of the patterns hidden in the tabernacle and the temple. Why was He teaching me about the Israelites' holy places of worship, I wondered, when what I had asked for was a deeper, more intimate relationship with Him?

It was not long before I had my answer: Because hidden in the patterns of the tabernacle and the temple is the pathway to His presence! And the more He has revealed to me about this pattern, the more intimacy I have experienced in my relationship with Him.

"Show the House to the House"

In the introduction, I mentioned that I was reading Ezekiel 43 one day and came across something that almost knocked me off my chair. God told Ezekiel,

Thou son of man, **show the house to the house** *of Israel, that they may be ashamed of their iniquities: and let them measure the pattern. And if they be ashamed of all that they have done, show them the form of the house...and*

write it in their sight, that they may keep the whole form thereof, and all the ordinances thereof, and do them. (Ezekiel 43:10–11 KJV)

God said, "*Show the house to the house.*" What was the first "*house*" to which God was referring? The temple! And what, or who, is the second "*house*"? The children of Israel! Why was Ezekiel to "*show the house to the house*"? So that the Israelites could understand the revelations of the pattern of the temple and be ashamed of their sin!

God was telling Ezekiel, in effect, "I've given you the pattern of My temple to follow. Now I want you to tell My people to look at this pattern, measure the pattern, and compare themselves to the pattern, so that they can be convicted of their sin and return to Me."

After reading this passage, I had a fresh revelation that the temple wasn't just a house of worship thousands of years ago in Old Testament times. The picture God painted of the temple in Scripture is for you and me *today*. There is a life-giving, life-changing, eternity-impacting purpose to its pattern.

You see, what happened under the old covenant was a blueprint for the new covenant, and together, the old and new covenants form a blueprint for us today. Paul told us that the things that happened to the children of Israel were to teach them *and* to teach us:

Now these things happened to them as an example, and they were written for our instruction, upon whom the ends of the ages have come. Therefore let him who thinks he stands take heed that he does not fall.

(1 Corinthians 10:11–12)

Remember, God uses the *natural* to reveal the *spiritual*.

God's Heavenly Tabernacle

Even though I had grown up as a preacher's kid and had read the Word over and over again, I had no idea there was a tabernacle in heaven. But, one day, God showed me that there is, in fact, a holy tabernacle in the heavenly realm—the very one that provided the pattern for the Israelites' earthly tabernacle in the wilderness!

The writer of Hebrews said, "*Just as Moses was warned by God when he was about to erect the tabernacle; for, 'SEE,' He says, 'THAT YOU MAKE all things ACCORDING TO THE PATTERN WHICH WAS SHOWN YOU ON THE MOUNTAIN'*" (Hebrews 8:5).

According to Scripture, God took Moses to the top of a mountain and showed him a pattern for how to build the tabernacle. To what mountain did God take him? It couldn't have been Mount Sinai, because there wasn't a tabernacle on Mount Sinai for Moses to see.

So, where was the mountain where God showed Moses the pattern? I believe that God took Moses to Mount Zion in a vision, showed him the temple in heaven, and then said, "*Let them construct a sanctuary for Me, that I may dwell among them. According to all that I am going to show you, as the pattern of the tabernacle and the pattern of all its furniture, just so you shall construct it*" (Exodus 25:8–9)!

Hebrews 9:23–24 also refers to the pattern (or the "copies") of heaven:

Therefore it was necessary for the copies of the things in the heavens to be cleansed with these, but the heavenly things themselves with better sacrifices than these. For Christ did not enter a holy place made with hands, a mere copy of the true one, but into heaven itself, now to appear in the presence of God for us.

In chapters 25 through 31 of Exodus, we read about the intricate plans for the tabernacle that God revealed to Moses, including the funding, building, furniture, coverings, priests, and sacrifices—details as minute as the pegs on which the serving utensils were to hang! Every item had meaning.

Moses was with God for forty days, observing and learning about the pattern, and when God had revealed all the details to him that he needed to complete the task, He sent Moses back to build the tabernacle according to the exact instructions he had been given.

To clarify, the *wilderness tabernacle*, constructed according to the plan God revealed to Moses on Mt. Sinai, was God's temporary dwelling place and the Israelites' house of worship during their exodus from Egypt. (See Reference figure L.) The *Jerusalem temple* was commissioned by Solomon, King David's son, to be the Israelites' "permanent" house of worship. However, it was destroyed by the Romans in 70 A.D., and all that remains is a portion of a wall, known today as the Wailing Wall. I'll share more with you about the temple in the next chapter.

Moses and Jesus

When Jesus was confronted by a group of religious Jews because He performed miracles on the Sabbath and claimed that God was His Father, He gave an amazing response to their accusations:

> *Do not think that I will accuse you before the Father; the one who accuses you is Moses, in whom you have set your hope.* **For if you believed Moses, you would believe Me; for he wrote of Me.** *But if you do not believe his writings, how will you believe My words?* (John 5:45–47)

Wait a second! Moses wrote about Jesus?

Moses wrote the first five books of the old covenant, known as the Torah: Genesis, Exodus, Leviticus, Numbers, and Deuteronomy. I have read these books and reread them and re-reread them, and I can assure you of one thing: The name of Jesus is not mentioned even once.

Why, then, did Jesus say, *"For if you believed Moses, you would believe Me; for he wrote about Me"*? Because Jesus is revealed in the pattern of the tabernacle!

When God showed Moses the pattern for building the tabernacle, there was significance far beyond the blueprint for a house of worship for God's people as they wandered in the wilderness. God was revealing a picture, a pattern, a plan, and a purpose for all future generations—a map to lead them into an intimate relationship with Him.

You Are the Temple

The pictures and pattern of the wilderness tabernacle and Solomon's temple have a tremendous impact on you and me today. The pictures God painted in His Word and the patterns He ordained thousands of years ago apply to us right now.

Paul wrote, *"Do you not know that your body is a temple of the Holy Spirit who is in you, whom you have from God, and that you are not your own? For you have been bought with a price: therefore glorify God in your body"* (1 Corinthians 6:19–20).

We don't belong to ourselves. We are God's, and He has a holy purpose for each of us. And not only are we the living tabernacle of God in which He now dwells; we also are priests serving the Most High God:

But you are A CHOSEN RACE, A *royal* PRIESTHOOD, A HOLY NATION, A PEOPLE FOR *God's* OWN POSSESSION, *that you may proclaim the excellencies of Him who has called you out of darkness into His marvelous light.*

(1 Peter 2:9)

God wants *all* of His children to know Him and to search out His ways. The goal of this book is to share with you the mysteries God has revealed to me throughout the last several years—mysteries that will help draw you into a more intimate relationship with Him.

As you continue on your journey toward intimacy with the Lord, I encourage you to dig deep into His Word to discover the rich storehouse of treasure He has laid up for you, both in this life and for all eternity.

Digging Deeper

1. God uses the *natural* to *reveal* the spiritual. Think of an example in your own life when He has used something in the natural world to teach you a spiritual truth.

2. James 4:8 promises, *"Draw near to God and He will draw near to you."* How near do you feel to God today? On a scale of 1 to 10, with 1 being completely alienated from God and 10 being enveloped by His loving presence, where would you place yourself?

3. Are you living *"as though you are not your own"* and as though *"your body is a temple of the Holy Spirit"*? Why or why not?

4. Spend time now talking with the Lord about your hunger—or lack thereof—for a more intimate relationship with Him. Ask Him to stir up a desire in you to dig deeper into His Word to discover the "gold" He has buried there for you.

8

FIRE AND GLORY

"The house that is to be built for the Lord shall be exceedingly magnificent, famous and glorious throughout all lands."
—1 Chronicles 22:5

When I cried out to God that I wanted to truly know Him, He gave me the five steps I shared in part I of this book: *repent, praise, worship, offering,* and *sacrifice.*

But His revelation didn't stop there. In fact, little did I know that what God had spoken to my spirit that morning in the hotel was only the beginning of the mysteries He wanted to reveal to me—mysteries that up until then had been veiled to my spiritual eyes and ears.

Over the course of the next several years, God surprised me with rich treasures buried in His Word, treasures of pictures and patterns hidden in the Old Testament about the wilderness tabernacle and Solomon's temple.

"Arise, Therefore, and Build"

As you may know, Solomon's temple was built following the pattern of Moses' tabernacle in the wilderness.

Even though King David knew he was not the one chosen to build the temple (see 2 Samuel 7), he still was passionate about the construction of God's house of worship in Jerusalem. He said, *"The house that is to be built for the LORD shall be exceedingly magnificent, famous and glorious throughout all lands. Therefore now I will make preparation for it"* (1 Chronicles 22:5).

Knowing that God had ordained his son Solomon to be crowned king after him, David was diligent to provide the resources needed to accomplish this monumental task. When David commissioned Solomon with the task of building the temple, he listed the provisions he had made ready for his son (see 1 Chronicles 22:14–15):

+ 100,000 talents of gold

+ 1,000,000 talents of silver

+ bronze and iron *"beyond weight"*

+ timber and stone

+ workmen, stonecutters, masons, carpenters, and skilled men

+ As a loving father, King David sternly admonished his son to remain faithful to the Lord in the construction process and throughout his reign:

Only the LORD give you discretion and understanding, and give you charge over Israel, so that you may keep the law of the LORD your God. Then you will prosper, if you are careful to observe the statutes and the ordinances which the LORD commanded Moses concerning Israel. Be strong and courageous, do not fear nor be dismayed. (1 Chronicles 22:12–13)

As a student of the Israelites' history and God's law, David knew that the blessings of God's presence, power, peace, protection, and prosperity were available only to those who walked in an obedient, faith-filled covenant relationship with Him. He also knew that, conversely, those who walked in disobedience and rebellion would receive God's judgment and the withdrawal of His covenant blessings.

Then David commanded Solomon,

Now set your heart and your soul to seek the LORD your God; arise, therefore, and build the sanctuary of the LORD God, so that you may bring the ark of the covenant of the LORD and the holy vessels of God into the house that is to be built for the name of the LORD. (1 Chronicles 22:19)

In the fourth year of his reign, around 960 B.C., King Solomon began building the temple on Mount Moriah in Jerusalem, and the construction continued for seven years, until it was finally completed, around 953 B.C. The site where Solomon chose to establish the temple was a place of tremendous historic significance to the Israelites.

The area of Mount Moriah is where Abraham encountered the high priest Melchizedek (see Genesis 14) and honored him by paying the first tithe recorded in Scripture. Years later, Abraham's faith was severely tested when he obeyed God by returning to Mt. Moriah with Isaac to offer his long-awaited promised son to the Lord as a sacrifice. (See Genesis 22.)

It was on Mount Moriah 900 years later when David repented for a serious sin by buying Araunah's threshing-room floor, building an altar on it, and offering God a sacrifice. (See 1 Chronicles 21:18–30; 2 Samuel 24:18–25.) Some historians also believe that it was near Mount Moriah that Jesus was crucified, which would serve as the prophetic fulfillment of Abraham's words to his son: *"God will provide for Himself the lamb"* (Genesis 22:8).

Mount Moriah was clearly a place that spoke of sacrifice to the Jewish people, and it was here that Solomon built this center of sacrifice and worship to the Most High God.

"Exceedingly Magnificent"

When the temple was completed, Solomon had all the furniture and articles that had been carefully designed and built put into place:

Thus all the work that Solomon performed for the house of the LORD was finished. And Solomon brought in the things that David his father had dedicated, even the silver and the gold and all the utensils, and put them in the treasuries of the house of God.   (2 Chronicles 5:1)

Once this was done, the most amazing worship service ever celebrated on earth began. *"So many sheep and oxen* [were sacrificed] *that they could not be counted or numbered"* (2 Chronicles 5:6). Then the priests and the Levites brought up the ark of the covenant from the temporary tent King David had erected and placed the ark in the Holy of Holies.

After the priests came out of the Most Holy Place, they began playing cymbals, stringed instruments, harps, trumpets, and other musical instruments, while all the Levites glorified the Lord and praised Him with thanksgiving, singing in unison, *"He indeed is good for His lovingkindness is everlasting"* (2 Chronicles 5:13).

As the glorious sounds of music and singing washed over all of Jerusalem, God responded to their worship with His manifested presence: *"Then the house, the house of the LORD, was filled with a cloud, so that the priests could not stand to minister because of the cloud, for the glory of the LORD filled the house of God"* (2 Chronicles 5:13–14).

Solomon then fell to his knees and prayed a passionate prayer dedicating the temple to God, which he concluded with this plea:

> *Now therefore arise, O LORD God, to Your resting place, You and the ark of Your might; let Your priests, O LORD God, be clothed with salvation and let Your godly ones rejoice in what is good. O LORD God, do not turn away the face of Your anointed; remember Your lovingkindness to Your servant David.*
>   (2 Chronicles 6:41–42)

When Solomon finished praying, fire came down from heaven and consumed the sacrifices and offerings, and the glory of the Lord filled the temple to such a degree that the priests could not even enter the building! In response to the fire and the glory, the Israelites fell on their faces before the Lord in worship. (See 2 Chronicles 7:1–3.)

This moment was the fulfillment of King David's heart's desire: Truly, the temple was an *"exceedingly magnificent, famous and glorious"* (1 Chronicles 22:5) house of worship to the Most High God.

You would think that after such a glorious, power-filled, life-changing experience, Solomon would have followed in his father's footsteps as a faithful worshipper of God all the days of his life. Sadly, this wasn't the case.

First Kings 11 tells the tragic story of how the wisest man who ever lived became the greatest of fools:

Solomon did what was evil in the sight of the LORD, and did not follow the LORD fully, as David his father had done. Then Solomon built a high place for Chemosh the detestable idol of Moab, on the mountain which is east of Jerusalem, and for Molech the detestable idol of the sons of Ammon. Thus also he did for all his foreign wives, who burned incense and sacrificed to their gods. Now the LORD was angry with Solomon because his heart was turned away from the LORD, the God of Israel, who had appeared to him twice, and had commanded him concerning this thing, that he should not go after other gods; but he did not observe what the LORD had commanded.

(1 Kings 11:6–10)

What follows is the beginning of the end of Solomon's reign. Rather than the glory and the fire being preserved and maintained in the temple throughout the generations of the Israelites, the rebellion of Solomon spilled on to God's chosen people and eventually resulted in the temple's destruction by King Nebuchadnezzar's Babylonian army less than four hundred years later.

However, the details of this glorious house of worship for the Most High God have been preserved forever in His Word, first in the explicit directions He gave to Moses for the construction of the wilderness tabernacle (see Exodus 26–31, 37–40), and then later in the detailed outline for the building of the temple (see 1 Kings 6–8; 2 Chronicles 2–7).

Next I want to share with you the details of the pictures and patterns hidden in Scripture, so that you, too, may have an increasingly intimate relationship with the Lord.

Digging Deeper

1. Consider the most powerful times of worship you've ever experienced. How do they compare to the worship service when Solomon dedicated the temple to the Lord?

2. The blessings of God's presence, power, peace, protection, and prosperity are available to all those who choose to walk in an obedient, faith-filled covenant relationship with Him. Does this describe your relationship with God?

3. In what areas of your life do you need to know and experience more of God's presence, power, peace, protection, and prosperity?

4. Spend time with the Lord, asking Him to show you anything that may be blocking you from receiving His blessings. If He reveals any sin or doubt, confess it and then ask for His courage, strength, and grace to walk intimately with Him in covenant relationship.

9

THE BEGINNING OF THE PATTERN

"Now these things happened to them as an example, and they were written
for our instruction."
—1 Corinthians 10:11

As children, many of us learned the Sunday school stories of the Exodus. We were taught how God sent Moses to tell Pharaoh, "Let my people go," and how God hardened Pharaoh's heart. We were told that God sent ten plagues against the people and the land of Egypt until finally Pharaoh relented and allowed the Israelites to leave. But there's much more to the story.

The Bible explains why God hardened Pharaoh's heart:

[God commanded Moses to tell Pharaoh,] *"For this reason I have allowed*
you to remain, in order to show you My power and in order to proclaim My
name through all the earth."…Then the LORD said to Moses, "Go to Pharaoh,
for I have hardened his heart and the heart of his servants, that I may perform
these signs of Mine among them, and that you may tell in the hearing of your

son, and of your grandson, how I made a mockery of the Egyptians, and how
I performed My signs among them; that you may know that I am the LORD."
(Exodus 9:16; 10:1–2)

Even while God was making a name for Himself, He was making a mockery
of the Egyptians as a spiritual representation of the world. Did you know that the
Bible describes how, literally hundreds of years after Israel left Egypt, the nations
Israel came into contact with had heard how God had delivered His people from
the hand of the Egyptians?

God Is Supreme

Why ten plagues? What's the significance? There were at least ten different
gods the Egyptians revered and worshipped.

1. When God used Moses to turn the water into blood, He was demonstrat-
    ing to the Egyptians that He was greater than Hapi, the god of the Nile.

2. When God brought the plague of frogs to overtake the land, He was
    demonstrating to the Egyptians that He was greater than Heqet, the
    goddess of the frogs.

3. When God caused lice to swarm the banks of the Nile and infect the
    Egyptian people, He was demonstrating to the Egyptians that He was
    greater than Kheper, their insect god.

4. When God brought the plague of flies to cover the land, He was again
    demonstrating to the Egyptians that He was greater than Kheper, their
    insect god.

5. When God brought a plague against the cattle and the Egyptians' cattle
    died, He was demonstrating to the Egyptians that He was greater than
    their bull god, Apis.

6. When God brought a plague of boils upon the Egyptian people, He was
    demonstrating to them that He was greater than their god of medicine,
    Imhotep.

7. When God brought the plague of hail and fire to destroy the Egyptians'
    crops, He was demonstrating to them that He was greater than Nut, the
    sky goddess.

8. When God brought the plague of locusts to infest Egypt and destroy the crops, He was demonstrating to them that He was greater than Min, the god of fertility and harvest.

9. When God brought a plague of darkness upon the Egyptian people, He was demonstrating to them that He was greater than their chief god of the sun, Ra.

10. And when God sent the death angel to kill the firstborn in the land, He was demonstrating to Pharaoh that He was greater than Pharaoh. You see, Pharaoh considered *himself* to be a god, as did the Egyptian people. His firstborn son was considered a god, as well. When Pharaoh's firstborn son died, God once again proved that He alone was supreme. Egypt had struck God's firstborn, the children of Israel. Now God would strike Egypt's firstborn.

Ten false gods. Ten plagues sent by the true God. Ten times God showed to the people He was more powerful than everything else they worshiped. Over and over again, God was saying, "I alone am God. There is none besides Me!"

God's People Are Distinct, Set Apart

When these plagues came against the land of Egypt, not one of them touched the land where the Israelites were living—not their crops; not their animals; not their families.

God spoke in Exodus 8:22–23, and said,

> But on that day I will set apart the land of Goshen, where My people are living, so that no swarms of insects will be there, in order that you may know that I, the LORD, am in the midst of the land. And I will put a division between My people and your people.

This is another revelation of the fact that God intends for His people to be separate—holy unto Him. Repeatedly throughout Exodus, God emphasizes the distinction between His people and the world.

Turn Your Back on All Other Gods

When Israel came out of Egypt, and God gave Moses the instructions for building the tabernacle, He told him that the main entrance to the outer court was to face the east. Why?

The "greatest" god the Egyptians worshipped was the sun god, Ra. We all know the sun rises in the east and sets in the west. God was saying to His people, "When you approach Me, when you come into My presence, you must turn your back on *all* other gods!

Like the Egyptians, we, too, may have many "gods" in our lives: money, power, fame, careers, relationships, drugs, alcohol, television, the Internet—anything we place over and above our relationship with God could be considered a god in our lives.

God says, "If you want to approach Me, if you want an intimate relationship with Me, if you want to experience and encounter My presence and power in your life, then you must turn your back on all other gods."

Enter the Encampment

In the first chapter of Numbers, God instructed Moses as to who (which tribe) was to camp and where (in relation to the tabernacle). Even the positioning of the tribes of Israel in relation to where they camped around the tabernacle had meaning, purpose, and revelation.

The tabernacle was to be pitched in the center of the camp of Israel. Everything else was arranged around it, in the same way that every part of our lives should revolve around God, the center.

Moses and Aaron were to camp closest to the east entrance to the tabernacle, followed by the tribes of Judah, Issachar, and Zebulun. These tribes guarded the entrance to the tabernacle. A casual observer might say, "No big deal; they had to camp somewhere." Yet there something more God is saying to us.

The tribe of Judah pitched their camp closest to the camps of Moses and Aaron. Many of us are familiar with the meaning of the word *Judah*: "May God be praised." The name *Issachar* means "He will bring reward." The Bible says of the tribe of Issachar that they were men who understood the times and knew what to do. (See 1 Chronicles 12:32.) And the name *Zebulun* means "dwelling, habitation."

May we be priests of God who understand the times we live in and know what must be done. May we bring our reward with us to God; may we praise Him; may we enter His dwelling and habitation!

The Tabernacle's Framework and Perimeter

Numbers are important to God, and He imparts them with significance throughout the Scriptures. God is a God of design, plan, and purpose—a truth that's clearly evidenced in the symbolism contained in the design and construction of the tabernacle.

The tabernacle consisted of three sections: the outer court, the inner court, and the Holy of Holies. In later chapters, we will explore the mysteries hidden in these areas. For now, consider the following numeric details:

- The framework for the tabernacle was made up of forty-eight boards overlaid with gold, and these boards stood in ninety-six sockets of silver. There is so much we could say about the meaning behind God's explicit instructions for the construction of the tabernacle—the number of boards; the sockets; the meaning behind the gold and silver—but, for the sake of our journey, I'm going to leave much of that for another time.

- The perimeter of the tabernacle was fifty cubits wide by one hundred cubits long, or approximately seventy-five feet by one hundred fifty feet. Forming the perimeter were fine linen cloths five cubits high, or approximately seven-an-a-half feet in height. The perimeter served as a demarcation between the people and the place of service and worship, as well as the very presence of God.

- The perimeter was supported by sixty columns, with silver on the top and brass on the bottom. Each of the columns was supported by two ropes, anchored into the ground to support the outer structure. Sixty is also the number of men in the bloodline from Adam to Jesus Christ. (See Matthew 1:1–16; Luke 3:23–38.)

- There were one hundred twenty ropes holding up the sixty posts. Before the flood, God gave mankind one hundred twenty years in which to repent.

(See Genesis 6:3.) Moses was one hundred twenty years old when he died. (See Deuteronomy 34:7.) In 2 Chronicles 5:11–14, there is reference to one hundred twenty priests blowing one hundred twenty silver trumpets. And there were one hundred twenty people in the upper room on the day of Pentecost. (See Acts 1:6–15.)

According to Jewish tradition, the ropes were referred to as *hands* and had names, the Word and the Spirit. It's the "hands" of the Word and the Spirit that hold up our lives. Without both, we are unstable and may topple over.

The number of columns, posts, ropes, sockets, gold, silver, and brass, as well as the dimensions of the entrances, all hold tremendous mysteries and revelation. Time doesn't permit a full exploration of these in this book, but in the next chapter, I will share with you the significance of the gates.

Digging Deeper

1. Having read about the ten gods the Egyptians worshipped—and there were probably many more than ten—consider whatever false "gods" you may be worshipping in your life. These could be material things, relationships, emotional ties, wrong thought patterns, or addictions—anything you may have been exalting above the one true God, whether knowingly or unknowingly.

2. Now, make a written list of your "gods," asking the Holy Spirit to reveal what is truly in your heart. Be courageous!

3. God has commanded us, *"You shall have no other gods before Me"* (Exodus 20:3). He is clear that His judgments and blessings are linked to our disobedience or obedience to this command, respectively. (See Exodus 20:3–6.) Are you ready to repent for anything or anyone you have exalted in your mind and heart over God? Be honest before the Lord and with yourself.

4. Spend time now talking to the Lord and confessing any struggle you may be having with false gods. After repenting, cry out for His mercy and grace in helping you to obey His command to have no other gods before Him. Then, praise and exalt Him as the one true God!

10

GUARDING YOUR GATES

"I have made a covenant with my eyes."
—Job 31:1

I n chapter 6, I shared with you that God has buried pictures and patterns within Scripture for us to discover. While it may be easier to just sit and read all the great stories in the Bible, we discover the vast richness buried in His Word only when we mine for the hidden "gold."

In coming chapters, we'll examine together the meaning behind the deep spiritual truths found in the natural reality of Moses' wilderness tabernacle. Together, we'll look at the structure of the outer court, the inner court, and the Holy of Holies, along with their contents, as we explore how they reveal an amazing pathway into the Lord's presence and His design for our lives.

I want you to keep all this in mind as we pause for a moment to look at Solomon's temple and the gates that were in the walls surrounding this holy house of sacrifice and worship. Now, you may be wondering, *Gates? What do gates have to do with an intimate relationship with the Lord?*

The psalmist declared, *"Enter His gates with thanksgiving and His courts with praise. Give thanks to Him, bless His name"* (Psalm 100:4). The pathway into the intimacy of God's presence begins with entering through the gates with His name on our lips and His praise in our hearts.

One Gate versus Five

As I noted earlier, Moses' wilderness tabernacle was the forerunner for Solomon's temple. While the layout of the tabernacle and temple are almost identical, there are a few differences. One of the primary distinctions has to do with the entrances.

Moses' tabernacle had only one entrance by which the outer court could be accessed. The picture painted for us in this detail is clear: There is only one way for us to enter into an intimate relationship with our heavenly Father.

Jesus said, *"I am the way, and the truth, and the life; no one comes to the Father but through Me"* (John 14:6). If we want access to God, we must enter through the one and only "gate" He has provided: Jesus Christ.

In the wall surrounding Solomon's temple mount, however, there were five gates. Biblical archaeologists have named them Barclay's Gate, the Double Gate, the Triple Gate, Warren's Gate, and the Eastern Gate.

Why five? Why not just one entryway, as with the tabernacle?

A practical reason for having more gates may have been because the number of Israelites had increased exponentially since the time when they had worshipped God in the wilderness. By the time they were assembling from all over the nation to worship at the temple in Jerusalem, there were more than five times as many Israelites, and so they probably needed five times as many entrances just to accommodate the crowds coming to offer their sacrifices and worship.

Another reason may have been that Solomon's temple, and the area surrounding it, was much bigger than the court of Moses' tabernacle. This, too, would necessitate more numerous entrances. Although we can only wonder about Solomon's reasoning in the natural, let's consider the spiritual significance behind the temple wall's five gates.

We know that in addition to Moses' God-given pattern of the tabernacle recorded in the Torah, King David received additional revelation from the Holy Spirit regarding how Solomon was to build the temple:

*Then David gave his son Solomon the plans for the vestibule, its houses, its treasuries, its upper chambers, its inner chambers, and the place of the mercy seat; and the plans for all that he had **by the Spirit**.*
(1 Chronicles 28:11–12 NKJV)

Since God revealed plans for the temple directly to David, we can safely assume that the wall had five gates leading to the temple mount simply because God *wanted* there to be five gates. The question is, why?

Watchmen on the Walls

The responsibilities of the hundreds of priests serving at the temple were varied, and in future chapters, I'll go into greater detail about some of their daily duties. For now, I want to focus exclusively on those priests who were in charge of the temple gates.

The first thing these priests did in the morning was to open the five gates, and the last thing they did at night was to close them. Night and day, there were shifts of priests assigned to stand guard on top of the temple wall and at the gates. These watchmen had three primary responsibilities:

1. Prohibit anything unclean from entering.
2. Blow the trumpets as a warning if the enemy was approaching.
3. Close the gates to keep out the enemy and protect the people.

The watchmen knew that these five gates were points of vulnerability through which the enemy could enter and potentially desecrate or destroy the temple. Should the watchmen abdicate their positions or fall asleep while on guard, the consequences could be immediate and severe.

According to ancient Jewish teaching, if a temple priest fell asleep while on watch, the consequences were severe: he was either beaten or shamed by being stripped naked and having his clothes burned. Jesus alluded to the consequences of falling asleep while on duty when He said, "*Behold, I am coming like a thief. Blessed is the one who stays awake and keeps his clothes, so that he will not walk about naked and men will not see his shame*" (Revelation 16:15).

So, what is the lesson God wants us to learn in the pattern of the five gates in Solomon's temple and the watchmen on the wall? To answer this question, let's look at the following two Scripture passages—one that the apostle Paul wrote to believers in Corinth, and one that Jesus' disciple Peter wrote to Christians living in Asia Minor.

Paul urged believers...

Flee immorality. Every other sin that a man commits is outside the body, but the immoral man sins against his own body. Or do you not know that your body is a temple of the Holy Spirit who is in you, whom you have from God, and that you are not your own? For you have been bought with a price: therefore glorify God in your body. (1 Corinthians 6:18–20)

And Peter wrote,

You also, as living stones, are being built up as a spiritual house for a holy priesthood, to offer up spiritual sacrifices acceptable to God through Jesus Christ. (1 Peter 2:5)

Do you see the amazing parallels between the temple gates and us, as believers?

- The temple was the dwelling place for God's Holy Spirit in the Israelites' camp. Now, as believers, we are the dwelling place of God's Holy Spirit.
- The tabernacle and the temple had three main sections: the outer court, the inner court, and the Holy of Holies. Our tabernacle, or temple, also has three sections: body, soul, and spirit.
- The priests were responsible for guarding and protecting the temple. Now, we are the priests who are responsible for guarding and protecting the "temple" of our bodies.
- The temple had five gates—and so do we! By "gates," I mean the orifices and body parts by which we exercise our five senses: eyes, ears, fingers/hands, nose, and mouth.

The only way to access the temple was to enter through one of the five gates into the courtyard. Then, if you were a priest, you would pass through to the outer court, the inner court, and, if you were the high priest, enter into the Holy of Holies. In the same way, we are "accessed" through one of the five "gates" of our body, and then through our soul, and finally through our spirit.

It is through our five "gates" that our five senses operate—by them, we see, hear, touch, smell, and taste! As God's appointed priests over our own bodies, it's our job to be the watchmen on the wall of our own "temple." Like the temple priests, it's our responsibility to...

1. Prohibit anything unclean from entering.

2. Heed the warning when the enemy is approaching.

3. Close the gates to protect ourselves from the enemy.

Sadly, most of us have done a poor job of guarding our own gates. We've...

+ Looked at things we definitely shouldn't have seen.

+ Listened to things we had no business hearing.

+ Touched things we clearly shouldn't have touched.

+ Consumed things God never intended for us to taste, let alone eat.

+ Spoken words that should never have come out of our mouths.

And we wonder why we're sick, poor, wretched, and blind. It's because we haven't stood watch as priests over our five gates and our temple—we've permitted the enemy to set up camp in our lives. But God has called us to be priests and watchmen on the walls of our temple. He has called us to stand guard against the enemy!

Guard Your Gates

Our hearts and minds are influenced, consciously and subconsciously, through whatever passes through the gates of our eyes, ears, hands, nose, and mouth. The failure to diligently guard the gates of our temple has had disastrous consequences for us, our families, our country, and, ultimately, the other nations of the world. This is because whoever or whatever controls our thoughts also governs the principles by which we live.

The gates of our eyes and ears probably have the greatest impact on our lives. The words and images we consistently see and hear, whether positive or negative, come in through our gates and become imbedded in our hearts and minds with little effort on our part.

According to Scripture, we are a reflection of what we think in our hearts: "For as [a person] *thinks within himself, so he is*" (Proverbs 23:7). Those things we continually expose ourselves to will eventually determine what we believe, how we think, the decisions we make, and how we live.

Personally, I don't believe anything has influenced our thoughts and actions more in the last fifty years than television. More recently, other forms of media have emerged, such as the Internet and cable and satellite television. Together, these have an alarming impact on our values, beliefs, morals, and behavior.

Why and how do the various forms of media have such control over us? Paul was a forward-thinking man. Consider what he wrote to the believers at Ephesus:

> *You were dead in your trespasses and sins, in which you formerly walked according to the course of this world, according to the **prince of the power of the air**, of the spirit that is now working in the sons of disobedience....For our struggle is not against flesh and blood, but against the rulers, against the powers, against the world forces of this darkness, against the spiritual forces of wickedness in the heavenly places.* (Ephesians 2:1–2; 6:12)

Paul was saying that the battles we fight in this life are not fought in the natural realm; rather, they are spiritual.

When we put all this together, we can see that our behavior, values, beliefs, and, ultimately, our relationship to God, are the result of what we have allowed to pass through the gates of our natural senses and into our spirits. We either will be influenced by God and His kingdom or by Satan, who is *"the prince of the power of the air."*

Clear the Air

A *prince* is a type of ruler. According to Ephesians 2:2, Satan is ruling the air and the power that's in it. Why? Because he realizes that whoever rules the air rules the earth. So, he has set up his headquarters in the air and made himself *"prince"* over it.

And what's in the air? Sound waves, light waves, microwaves, radio frequencies, satellite signals, broadcast transmissions, wireless transmissions, and so forth. This is what the media uses to send powerful messages all over the world. The word *media* means "middle," and the sad truth is that media...

+ Stands in the middle between the source of the messages and those targeted to receive it.

+ Serves as the conduit to carry the message from where it originates to the person who watches, hears, or reads it.

+ Is one of the enemy's most effective tools in Satan's arsenal against humanity.

Satan realizes that whoever controls the media—music, television, movies, newspapers, magazines, the Internet, and so on—will rule our hearts. This is why advertisers spend billions of dollars each year on marketing campaigns aimed to influence our thoughts and choices.

What we once called "morally unacceptable" is now broadcast on prime time television every night. What the Bible calls "sin" is now considered an "alternative lifestyle." Any efforts to take a stand for scriptural principles are labeled "censorship" and "intolerance."

The enemy is determined to control the images and sounds that are broadcast into our homes, and because of this, media's messages of darkness have torn at the fabric of society. Satan's goal is to fill the airwaves with violence, perversity, and immorality so that he can penetrate the "gates" of our eyes and ears, thereby gaining access to our hearts and minds, in his effort to steal, kill, and destroy our very lives. (See John 10:10.)

The messages seen and heard through media shape our minds and hearts for good or evil, and every family has been affected by the spiritual darkness attempting to invade our homes. Every time we turn on the television, listen to the radio, or use the Internet, we're potentially inviting this spiritual battle right into our homes.

That is why it's imperative that we guard the gates of our own temple—and, as parents and grandparents, that we guard the temple gates of our children and grandchildren—against the enemy's advances.

Tragically, most of us have become numb to this spiritual darkness. Instead of being watchmen on the wall, too many of us have swung wide the gates of our eyes and ears, inviting the enemy to come on in and make himself at home. We've become like the proverbial frog swimming contentedly in the pot of water that's gradually heating on the stove. The frog is unaware that it's being cooked until it's too late.

In the same way, the strategy by which the enemy numbs us to the evil around us is gradual and subtle. The first time we're exposed to something ungodly, we're disgusted. The second time, we react negatively, but we aren't not quite as shocked. The third time, we watch a little bit more. The fourth time, we watch the whole thing. The fifth time, we're actually using the television remote to look for violent or lustful content to entertain and excite us.

Before we know it, media's darkness has moved through the gates of our eyes and ears and has infiltrated our hearts and minds. This is how Satan uses his seductive powers of the air. Like the temple guards, we must stay awake and not be found sleeping on the job so that we will not be shamed by the enemy!

Cover Your Eyes

I don't know any parents who would knowingly hire as a babysitter someone with a filthy mouth or a blatant disrespect for authority; someone who speaks, acts, and dresses in a sexually suggestive manner. However, this is exactly what we do when we allow negative forms of media to entertain and occupy our children's time and attention. Alarming studies reveal that…

- By the time he or she graduates from high school, the average child has watched 18,000 hours of TV.
- The average child in the United States will witness an astonishing 200,000 violent acts on television by the age of eighteen.
- More than 300,000 pornographic Web sites now *specifically* target children and teens.
- On average, children are spending 6.5 hours a day engaged with TV, the Internet, digital games, radio, and mp3 players or iPods.
- By the time they finish elementary school, most children will have spent more time watching TV than they will spend with their fathers over the course of their entire lifetime!

The impact of these statistics is devastatingly clear. Families are being torn apart by divorce, drug abuse, teen pregnancy, abortion, crime, violence, hatred, and so much more. What was once an invading spirit of darkness has now become a resident spirit of darkness.

The root of the problem is that, unlike Job and David, most of us haven't made a "covenant with our eyes." Job knew that in order to avoid temptation, he needed to guard the gate of his eyes:

I have made a covenant with my eyes; how then could I gaze at a virgin? And what is the portion of God from above or the heritage of the Almighty from on high? Is it not calamity to the unjust, and disaster to those who work iniquity? (Job 31:1–3)

David also vowed,

I will set no worthless thing before my eyes; I hate the work of those who fall away; it shall not fasten its grip on me. A perverse heart shall depart from me; I will know no evil. (Psalm 101:3–4)

David had experienced firsthand the disastrous consequences of failing to diligently guard the gate of his eyes when his wandering gaze led to an adulterous affair with Bathsheba. (See 2 Samuel 11.)

We must guard our five gates and refuse to admit anything unclean into our body, soul, or spirit. When the Holy Spirit warns us of the enemy's advance, we must respond immediately by barring his access to our heart and mind. Like Job and David, we must vow not to watch, listen to, smell, touch, or taste anything that is displeasing to God and disobedient to His Word.

How do we determine what *should* be permitted access to our heart and mind? It's easy!

Whatever is true, whatever is honorable, whatever is right, whatever is pure, whatever is lovely, whatever is of good repute, if there is any excellence and if anything worthy of praise, dwell on these things. (Philippians 4:8)

Proactive Priests

God has called each of us to be the priest over our own temple. We are not victims! As we choose to guard our gates and stand firm against Satan's temptations, he will be impotent to use the media or anything else to influence our behavior, our values, our beliefs, and our relationship with God.

Failure to stand firm against Satan's strategies not only brings disaster to our lives; it also blocks us from experiencing intimacy with the Lord. God is holy, and He requires holiness of all those who desire to spend time in His presence.

> *As obedient children, do not be conformed to the former lusts which were yours in your ignorance, but like the Holy One who called you, be holy yourselves also in all your behavior.* (1 Peter 1:14–15)

The only way we can be made holy is through the blood of Jesus Christ, which we will discuss in greater detail in the next chapter. For now, know that once Jesus' blood covers and purifies our sin natures, we are responsible before God for maintaining our purity through our choices and actions.

> *Who may ascend into the hill of the* LORD? *And who may stand in His holy place? He who has clean hands and a pure heart, who has not lifted up his soul to falsehood and has not sworn deceitfully. He shall receive a blessing from the* LORD *and righteousness from the God of his salvation.* (Psalm 24:3–5)

Keep in mind, however, that all efforts to maintain our purity simply by zealously watching over our gates will eventually become nothing more than religious striving and futile attempts to obey self-imposed rules; and, according to God's Word, striving to obey religious laws ultimately results in failure. (See Romans 7.) However, when we…

- rely on God and His Word to overcome temptation (see Psalm 119:11),
- know that He will deliver us from all temptation (see Matthew 6:13),
- trust that Christ in us is our hope of glory (see Colossians 1:27),
- believe we can do all things through Him who gives us strength (see Philippians 4:13),
- endeavor to walk in the power of the Holy Spirit (see Galatians 5:16),

♦ resist the devil so that he will flee from us (see James 4:7),

♦ and choose to glorify God with our bodies (see 1 Corinthians 6:19–20),

...then we are empowered to continue on the pathway leading to God's glorious and intimate presence, walking in the righteousness of Jesus Christ alone.

Let's continue now on our journey and discover how the wonder-working power of Jesus' blood is vital in our pursuit of intimacy with Him.

Digging Deeper

1. When you were growing up, how effective were your parents, grandparents, or other guardians as watchmen on the wall to protect your five gates from the enemy's access? How did this impact you?

2. How effective have you been as an adult in serving as the priest over your temple? Have you consistently chosen to glorify God with your body?

3. What do you sense the Holy Spirit may be leading you to do in order to be more diligent in guarding your gates?

4. Read and meditate on the following Scriptures: Psalm 119:9–16; Galatians 5:16–25; James 4:7–10; 1 Corinthians 6:18–20.

5. Spend some time talking to the Lord about what you can do to serve Him more faithfully as the priest of your temple. Ask His Holy Spirit to reveal the ways in which you have neglected to do this, and then repent. Finally, thank God for leading you on His pathway to intimacy.

11

THERE'S POWER IN THE BLOOD!

"Behold, the Lamb of God who takes away the sin of the world!"
—John 1:29

F rom the very beginning of God's relationship with man, He ordained the power of a blood sacrifice. Abel was part of the very first family, and God was pleased when he brought Him a sacrifice from his flock of sheep: *"Abel, on his part also brought of the firstlings of his flock and of their fat portions. And the LORD had regard for Abel and for his offering"* (Genesis 4:4).

As God's covenant relationship with His people deepened and expanded through the generations, blood sacrifices continued to be at the center of their worship. Noah, Abraham, Isaac, and Jacob all honored God with blood sacrifices; and while all of these were significant, the most profound blood sacrifice in the Old Testament was the killing of the Passover lamb.

Saved by the Blood of a Lamb

Although God had used Moses and Aaron to bring nine terrible plagues on the Egyptians, Pharaoh still refused to let the Israelites go. So, God commanded a tenth plague: the killing of all the firstborn throughout Egypt. No one would escape this horrifying judgment except those Jews who carefully obeyed God's instructions:

> *Then Moses called for all the elders of Israel and said to them, "Go and take for yourselves lambs according to your families, and slay the Passover lamb. You shall take a bunch of hyssop and dip it in the blood which is in the basin, and apply some of the blood that is in the basin to the lintel and the two doorposts; and none of you shall go outside the door of his house until morning. For the LORD will pass through to smite the Egyptians; and when He sees the blood on the lintel and on the two doorposts, the LORD will pass over the door and will not allow the destroyer to come in to your houses to smite you."*
> (Exodus 12:21–23)

Just as God had warned, at midnight, every firstborn child and animal throughout the land was struck dead, from Pharaoh's household to the prisoners in the dungeon. (See Exodus 12:29.) Only those protected by the blood of the Passover lamb were saved.

God instituted Passover as an everlasting celebration when He spoke these words: *"Now this day will be a memorial to you, and you shall celebrate it as a feast to the LORD; throughout your generations you are to celebrate it as a permanent ordinance"* (Exodus 12:14). Ever since that night, faithful Jews and believers around the world have observed the Feast of the Passover to commemorate the night when God "passed over" their homes and families, sparing them from the plague of death.

Years later, when God commanded Moses to construct the tabernacle and its contents according to the pattern He had provided (see Exodus 25:40), He instituted blood sacrifices as part of the Israelites' daily worship. God made it clear to the Israelites why blood sacrifices were required:

> *For the life of the flesh is in the blood, and I have given it to you on the altar to make atonement for your souls; for it is the blood by reason of the life that makes atonement.*
> (Leviticus 17:11)

The Hebrew word for *"atonement"* is *chaphar*, which means "to cover, make reconciliation, appease, purge, or cleanse." God's holiness requires a blood sacrifice to "cover" sin. Because the blood contains the essence of life, its value cannot be overstated.

Let's continue now on our pathway into the intimacy of God's presence and move beyond the gates and into the outer court of Moses' wilderness tabernacle, which, as you will discover, was a very bloody place.

The Bronze Altar in the Natural

The outer court of the tabernacle was a large rectangle measuring 100 cubits long by 50 cubits wide by 5 cubits high (its footprint was approximately 11,250 square feet), formed by curtains hanging from rods suspended on pillars. God designed the tabernacle to be portable, so that it could be dismantled and carried as the Israelites traveled through the desert.

When the people entered the outer court, the first thing they saw was the bronze altar. According to God's instructions in Exodus 27:1–8, the altar was...

+ made of acacia, a very hard and durable wood.

+ overlaid with bronze.

+ seven-and-a-half feet long by seven-and-a-half feet wide, and four-and-a-half feet deep.

The bronze altar had...

+ a bronze grate inside, on which the sacrifice was laid.

+ bronze utensils made specifically for use with the altar.

+ four horns on each of the four top corners.

+ a ring on each of the four corners, with two poles inserted through it, for carrying the altar through the wilderness.

+ a continuously burning fire.

Leviticus 1–7 describes five different kinds of offerings that were sacrificed to God on the bronze altar, four of which were blood sacrifices. Two of these five offerings were mandatory and were offered as atonement for the sins of the people: the sin offering and the trespass offering.

When atonement for sin was required, the male head of the house brought a spotless goat or a lamb to the priests. (See Leviticus 4:27–35; 5:5–13.) Before it was killed, the animal was tied to one of the altar's horns, and the person who had brought the offering laid his hands on the animal's head, to symbolize that his sins and the sins of his family were being transferred onto this blood sacrifice.

After the animal was killed, if it was a sin offering, the priest dipped his finger in the blood and applied it to the horns of the altar. If it was a trespass offering, the blood was sprinkled on the side of the altar. The remaining blood from both offerings was poured out on the altar's base. The goat or lamb was then placed on the altar and roasted, so that the priests could eat the meat.

The Hebrew word for *priest* is *kohen*, which means "officiating." The priests spent their lives serving God and attending to the responsibilities of the tabernacle and, eventually, the temple. They were needed to officiate at the sacrifices and offer the blood to God as a covering for the people's sin. If there had been no blood sacrifices, there would have been no need for an altar, no need for a tabernacle, and no need for the priests. Everything in the tabernacle centered on the blood sacrifices offered there throughout the day.

According to Exodus 29:38–42, the priests began the daily ritual sacrifices by killing a lamb as a sin offering to the Lord and burning it on the bronze altar. The sacrifices continued throughout the morning and afternoon, until the final sacrifice of the day, which was another lamb given as a sin offering.

The busyness of the activity, the noise of all the animals, the stench of the blood, and the smell of the burning meat must have been overwhelming. As difficult as it may be for us to understand in the twenty-first century, the blood sacrifices performed in the tabernacle's outer court were a vital step on the pathway leading into the Holy of Holies, where God's presence resided.

Now that we've looked at the natural picture of the bronze altar and the outer court sacrifices made there, let's dig deeper to discover the "gold" of their spiritual significance.

A Closer Look at the Bronze Altar

One of the priest's daily responsibilities was clearing away the ashes from the sacrifices burned on the previous day. This was necessary because the fire was never to be allowed to burn out, and accumulated ashes would have prevented oxygen from getting to the fire and allowing it to burn steadily. Too many ashes would have extinguished the flame because the fire wouldn't have been able to "breathe."

What is the spiritual picture God wants us to see here?

The previous day's ashes from the bronze altar represent the past. So many of us haven't scraped off the "ashes" of our past from the altar of our lives. We're holding on to bitterness, anger, and resentment from old wounds, and we refuse to let go as we tightly hold on to the grudges we bear from past offenses.

Through the pattern of the bronze altar, God is saying to us, "Scrape away those dead ashes. Allow My love to heal your pain. Forgive those who have hurt and wounded you. Repent of your unforgiveness. Cover all of it with the sacrificial blood of My Son, so that the breath of My Holy Spirit can blow again over the flame of your heart."

As you choose to forgive, repent, and let go of the past, the love of God, the powerful blood of Jesus Christ, and the gentle wind of the Holy Spirit will bring you to a place of freedom in Him that you've never experienced before. His joy and peace will flood your soul, and you will be set free to move forward on your pathway into God's presence.

The Spiritual Significance of the Altar's Four Sides

As described in Exodus 27, the bronze altar had four sides, and I want us to take a closer look at the spiritual picture that I believe each of these paints for us today.

1. The first side of the altar represents the forgiveness of our past sins.

For all have sinned and fall short of the glory of God, being justified as a gift by His grace through the redemption which is in Christ Jesus; whom God displayed publicly as a propitiation in His blood through faith. This was to demonstrate His righteousness, because in the forbearance of God He passed over the sins previously committed. (Romans 3:23–25)

2. The second side of the bronze altar represents our old nature, the "old man," who has passed away.

Knowing this, that our old self was crucified with Him, in order that our body of sin might be done away with, so that we would no longer be slaves to sin.
(Romans 6:6)

Therefore if anyone is in Christ, he is a new creature; the old things have passed away; behold, new things have come. (2 Corinthians 5:17)

3. The third side of the bronze altar represents the breaking of sin's hold over us.

For the death that He died, He died to sin once for all; but the life that He lives, He lives to God. Even so consider yourselves to be dead to sin, but alive to God in Christ Jesus. Therefore do not let sin reign in your mortal body so that you obey its lusts, and do not go on presenting the members of your body to sin as instruments of unrighteousness; but present yourselves to God as those alive from the dead, and your members as instruments of righteousness to God. (Romans 6:10–12)

4. The fourth side of the bronze altar represents the offering of our lives to God.

Therefore I urge you, brethren, by the mercies of God, to present your bodies a living and holy sacrifice, acceptable to God, which is your spiritual service of worship. And do not be conformed to this world, but be transformed by the renewing of your mind, so that you may prove what the will of God is, that which is good and acceptable and perfect. (Romans 12:1–2)

Just as the bronze altar was the first piece of furniture encountered in the tabernacle, so is the cross of Jesus Christ the first thing we must encounter on our pathway into intimacy with the Lord. God's requirement for a blood sacrifice to atone for our sins continues to this day.

Now that we've looked at the spiritual picture of what the bronze altar represented, let's turn our attention to the picture of the animal sacrifices and their prophetic implication.

Jesus, Our Passover Lamb

The bronze altar and the animal sacrifices were a prophetic sign of the sacrificial death of Jesus Christ as the final atonement for our sins. The prophet Isaiah foretold how the Messiah would be slaughtered like a Passover lamb:

He was oppressed and He was afflicted, yet He did not open His mouth; like a lamb that is led to slaughter, and like a sheep that is silent before its shearers, so He did not open His mouth. (Isaiah 53:7)

The Israelites' animal sacrifices were symbolic of God's grace meeting man's need for redemption. Likewise, Jesus' sacrificial death on the cross portrays the extravagant mercy God has extended to us. Because there was no sin in Jesus, He became our spotless Passover lamb.

John the Baptist recognized this truth when he pointed to Jesus and declared, *"Behold, the Lamb of God who takes away the sin of the world!"* (John 1:29). Like the Jews at the first Passover, only those of us whose sins are covered by the blood of the Lamb will be spared eternal death at the hands of the destroyer.

As we read in Leviticus 17:11, *"The life of the flesh is in the blood."* The writer of Hebrews powerfully underscored the prophetic implication of the tabernacle sacrifices:

*For when every commandment had been spoken by Moses to all the people according to the Law, he took the blood of the calves and the goats, with water and scarlet wool and hyssop, and sprinkled both the book itself and all the people, saying, "*THIS IS THE BLOOD OF THE COVENANT WHICH GOD COMMANDED YOU.*" And in the same way he sprinkled both the tabernacle and all the vessels of the ministry with the blood. And according to the Law, one may almost say, all things are cleansed with blood, and **without shedding of blood there is no forgiveness.*** (Hebrews 9:19–22)

The power of the blood Jesus shed on the cross for us is reinforced again and again throughout the New Testament:

- *"You were not redeemed with perishable things like silver or gold from your futile way of life inherited from your forefathers, but with precious blood, as of a lamb unblemished and spotless, **the blood of Christ***" (1 Peter 1:18–19).

+ "In Him we have redemption through **His blood**, the forgiveness of our trespasses, according to the riches of His grace" (Ephesians 1:7).

+ "But now in Christ Jesus you who formerly were far off have been brought near by **the blood of Christ**" (Ephesians 2:13).

+ "For it was the Father's good pleasure for all the fullness to dwell in Him, and through Him to reconcile all things to Himself, having made peace through **the blood of His cross**" (Colossians 1:19–20).

+ "But if we walk in the Light as He Himself is in the Light, we have fellowship with one another, and **the blood of Jesus** His Son cleanses us from all sin" (1 John 1:7).

Just as the priest couldn't bypass the altar to access the Holy of Holies, we can't bypass Jesus to get to God. Sadly, many people today mistakenly believe the lie that there is more than one way to God. Jesus said, "*I am the way, and the truth, and the life; no one comes to the Father but through Me*" (John 14:6). Jesus didn't say that He was one of many ways to God. He didn't say He was "a" way, "a" truth, or "a" life. No, He said, "*I am **the** way, **the** truth, and **the** life.*" He was very clear that no one can come to the Father except through Him.

It's vital for us to remember that the ultimate purpose of the blood sacrifices performed in the tabernacle was to make atonement for the Israelites' sins and lead them to God. This is still true today. Without a blood sacrifice, we cannot enter into God's presence. If there is no blood, there is no atonement for our sin, and if there is no atonement for our sin, then there can be no intimacy with Him.

Keep in mind, too, that the sacrifices offered by the priest on the bronze altar had to be performed again and again and again. However, the blood sacrifice of Jesus was the final atonement for our sins. Once He was crucified on our behalf, God's requirement for blood sacrifices was fulfilled, once and for all.

Every priest stands daily ministering and offering time after time the same sacrifices, which can never take away sins; but He, having offered one sacrifice for sins for all time, SAT DOWN AT THE RIGHT HAND OF GOD, waiting from that time onward UNTIL HIS ENEMIES BE MADE A FOOTSTOOL FOR HIS FEET. For by one offering He has perfected for all time those who are sanctified. (Hebrews 10:11–14)

Thankfully, we don't need to go forward every Sunday to the altar rail to get saved again and again. When we invite Jesus Christ to be our Lord and Savior, His blood cleanses us from our sin, and we are forever freed to walk in a loving, obedient, faith-filled covenant relationship with Him.

Washed Whiter than Snow

Do you remember how I shared with you that the first word God gave me in the hotel room was *repent*? In response to my heart's cry to truly know Him, God was just beginning to reveal the pattern of the tabernacle to me. He wanted me to understand that just as the Israelites had to repent with a blood sacrifice in order to approach Him, so I needed to come before Him in repentance, trusting in the blood of Jesus Christ to atone for my sins.

Not only do we need to repent for our sin nature, but, as I shared with you, we also need to repent continually of the sins we commit each day. Yes, we're saved. Yes, we're washed clean by Jesus' blood. But Jesus taught us that every day, we must repent of our daily trespasses that can keep us separated from God's presence. (See Matthew 6:9–13.) It's one thing to be saved by the power of the blood; it's another thing to be forgiven for our daily trespasses.

God says in His Word, *"Behold, the LORD's hand is not so short that it cannot save; nor is His ear so dull that it cannot hear. But your iniquities have made a separation between you and your God"* (Isaiah 59:1–2).

Oftentimes, we're waiting patiently for God to do something for us, but there is unrepented sin in our lives that is blocking the release of His blessings. Too many people falsely believe that they're under a cloud of grace that gives them license to do whatever they want, as long as they ask God to forgive them. Yet there are consequences of our choices, and we can't choose to live in disobedience to God's Word and expect to have intimacy with Him.

Whom does God welcome into His presence?

He who has clean hands and a pure heart, who has not lifted up his soul to falsehood and has not sworn deceitfully. He shall receive a blessing from the LORD and righteousness from the God of his salvation. (Psalm 24:4–5)

As believers, you and I have been washed clean by the blood of the Lamb. I urge you to claim the power of His blood over your life each day as you repent of your trespasses and walk in His victory over the power of sin.

You know, I love to worship the Lord, and while I really appreciate the contemporary worship songs we sing in church, there's something special to me about the old hymns. The theological truths they contain are powerful. One of my favorites is "There Is Power in the Blood," written by Lewis E. Jones in 1899.

Would you be free from the burden of sin?
   There's power in the blood, power in the blood;
Would you o'er evil a victory win?
   There's wonderful power in the blood.
There is power, power, wonder working power
   In the blood of the Lamb;
There is power, power, wonder working power
   In the precious blood of the Lamb.

Would you be whiter, much whiter than snow?
   There's power in the blood, power in the blood;
Sin stains are lost in its life giving flow.
   There's wonderful power in the blood.

My friend, there *is* power in the blood of Jesus Christ! Power to save. Power to free. Power to change. Power to restore. Power to redeem. Power!

God's Pattern of Redemption

Without shedding of blood there is no forgiveness.   (Hebrews 9:22)

Like the garment Jesus had worn just before His crucifixion (see John 19:23), the Bible is one seamless whole. The pattern established from the beginning and revealed in the tabernacle and the temple was fulfilled in Jesus, in whose blood is power to give us victory and to free us from sin's destructive hold.

Let me explain this pattern. Twice a day—every morning at nine o'clock and every evening at three—the high priest would offer a lamb as a sin offering. These daily offerings were called the *tamid*. On feast days like Passover, three lambs were sacrificed: one at 9 a.m., the second at noon, and the third at 3 p.m.

One of the duties of the high priest was to inspect the lamb to make sure there were no spots or blemishes. It had to be a perfect lamb. Once the lamb had been sacrificed, the high priest would stand next to the bronze altar and wait until the sacrifice was completed. Then, he would raise his hands and stretch out his arms, declaring, "It is finished!"

Are you beginning to see the pattern? But there's more.

According to Mark 15:25, Jesus was crucified at the third hour (or 9 a.m., since 6 a.m. was considered the first hour). Then, Mark 15:34 tells us that at the *"ninth hour"*—3 p.m., the exact time the high priest was standing over the sacrifice of the Passover lamb; the exact time the high priest was declaring, "It is finished!"—Jesus, the Lamb of God, our Passover Lamb, with outstretched arms on a cross, having paid the price for the penalty of our sins, took His final breath and cried out, *"It is finished!"* (John 19:30).

Digging Deeper

1. Some people find it offensive, distasteful, or even cruel that God requires a blood sacrifice in order to come into His presence. Is this difficult for you to accept? Why or why not?

2. As you consider the spiritual picture God has painted for us in the ashes on the bronze altar, ask Him if there is any bitterness, anger, or resentment from your past or present that may be preventing you from moving into a place of deeper intimacy with Him.

3. What areas of your life are covered with the wonder-working power of Jesus' blood? In what areas do you still need to apply His blood so that you are freed from the power of sin?

4. Spend time with God, thanking Him for sacrificing His Son as your Passover Lamb. Ask Him to reveal any areas of your life—past or present—where you need to apply Jesus' wonder-working blood, so that you can walk in victory over sin. Praise Him for all that He has done and is doing in your life.

12

WASHED BY THE WATER
AND THE WORD

"We all, with unveiled face, beholding as in a mirror the glory of the Lord,
are beingtransformed into the same image from glory to glory, just as
from the Lord, the Spirit."
—2 Corinthians 3:18

After the bronze altar, the bronze laver was the next piece of furniture encountered in the outer court of the tabernacle, and it was placed between the altar and the entrance leading to the inner court. (See Reference figure A-1.) God gave Moses the following instructions for the building of the laver:

You shall also make a laver of bronze, with its base of bronze, for washing; and you shall put it between the tent of meeting and the altar, and you shall put water in it. Aaron and his sons shall wash their hands and their feet from it; when they enter the tent of meeting, they shall wash with water, so that they will not die; or when they approach the altar to minister, by offering up in smoke a fire sacrifice to the LORD. So they shall wash their hands and their feet, that they may not die; and it shall be a perpetual statute for them, for Aaron and his descendants throughout their generations.   (Exodus 30:18–21)

From Exodus 38:8, we learn that the laver was made from the bronze mirrors of the women who served at the tabernacle. Since there was no glass in biblical times, one of the only reflective surfaces they had was highly polished brass. The women would polish small pieces of brass until they became like a shiny mirror, and these were the mirrors Moses used to make the bronze laver.

After the work on the tabernacle was completed and all the pieces of the furniture were ready to be installed, God gave Moses instructions for consecrating everything to Him, including how to dedicate Aaron and his sons, who were appointed to serve as priests. God commanded Moses to wash them in water from the bronze laver and anoint them with oil:

And you shall anoint the laver and its stand, and consecrate it. Then you shall bring Aaron and his sons to the doorway of the tent of meeting and wash them with water. You shall put the holy garments on Aaron and anoint him and consecrate him, that he may minister as a priest to Me. You shall bring his sons and put tunics on them; and you shall anoint them even as you have anointed their father, that they may minister as priests to Me; and their anointing will qualify them for a perpetual priesthood throughout their generations.   (Exodus 40:11–15)

Our English word *laver* comes from the ancient Latin word *lavare*, which means "to pour water on, to wash." Although this consecration of the high priest was the initial use for the bronze laver, all the priests were required by God's law to wash in its water throughout the day before entering the inner court and the Holy of Holies.

Because the priests' hands would be bloody from performing the daily sacrifices and their feet dirty from the bare ground on which the tabernacle stood, God's holiness demanded that they wash their hands and feet at the bronze laver. If a priest bypassed the laver without washing, the penalty was death. (See Exodus 30:20.) That's how important the bronze laver was to God!

Another of the priests' jobs was to wash the sacrifices after the animals had been slaughtered and before they were placed on the altar. (See Leviticus 1:8, 13.) As we

A-1

A-2

B-1

B-2

C-1

C-2

Mercury

Venus

Earth

Mars

Sizes in relation to Earth's surrounding planets

Jupiter

Mercury

Earth

Venus

Mars

Sun

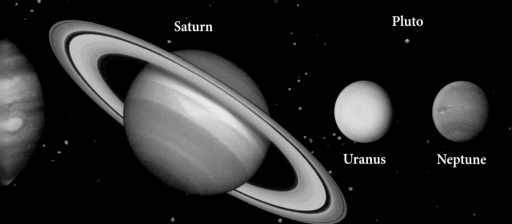

Saturn

Pluto

Uranus

Neptune

Planet sizes in relation to the Sun

Star sizes in relation to the Sun

Pollux

Sirius

Sun

Arcturus

Stars in relation to Antares

Arcturus

Sirius

Pollux

Arcturus

Antares

Aldebaran

Rigel

learned in the previous chapter, *"the life of the flesh is in the blood"* (Leviticus 17:11), and God had forbidden the priests from eating blood (see Leviticus 17:10, 12), so the sacrifices had to be washed in the bronze laver, as well.

What Does It All Mean?

The natural picture of the bronze laver would be nothing more than a few interesting biblical facts if it weren't for the spiritual pattern God wants us to learn from its construction and use.

The bronze laver is a picture of the cleansing that comes to us as we are washed daily by the Word of God. In his letter to the believers in Ephesus, Paul wrote of Jesus Christ sanctifying us by the *"washing of water with the word"* (Ephesians 5:26), so that He might present us before God as His pure, spotless bride.

It's one thing for us to be redeemed by Christ's death on the cross. Theologians call that *justification*. When I went to Sunday school as a boy, I can remember my teacher breaking down that big word, difficult to understand, into a simple explanation I have never forgotten: "I'm justified, 'just-as-if I'd' never sinned."

It's another thing altogether for us to be *sanctified*. To sanctify someone means to dedicate him by setting him apart and making him holy. At the bronze altar, we are justified (made righteous), and our sins are forgiven by the blood of our sacrificial Lamb. But at the bronze laver, we're sanctified and set apart for God's service.

When Jesus was crucified, the Roman soldiers pierced His side with a spear to make sure He was dead. When they did, blood *and* water poured from Jesus' body! (See John 19:31–35.) What a picture this is of how we must receive His sacrificial blood *and* be sanctified by water in the outer court if we desire to journey into a place of deep intimacy with the Lord.

> *And who is the one who overcomes the world, but he who believes that Jesus is the Son of God? This is the One who came by water and blood, Jesus Christ; not with the water only, but with the water and with the blood. It is the Spirit who testifies, because the Spirit is the truth. For there are three that testify: the Spirit and the water and the blood; and the three are in agreement.*
>
> (1 John 5:5–8)

Atonement for our sins is made possible through the blood on the bronze altar, and sanctification for our souls is made possible through the water of the bronze laver.

"My Beloved Son"

The bronze laver is also a picture of water baptism. The word *baptism* comes from the Greek word *baptizo*, which means "to wash, to cover with water, to moisten." At the start of Jesus' ministry here on earth, He was baptized by His cousin John in the Jordan River. As He came up out of the water, the Holy Spirit fell on Him, and God spoke from heaven, saying, *"This is My beloved Son, in whom I am well-pleased"* (Matthew 3:17).

Of course, Jesus wasn't cleansed or made holy through His baptism; He was the only sinless Person ever to walk the earth, and, as such, He didn't need to be made clean. God used water baptism to symbolize that His Son was being set apart so that He could fulfill His God-given destiny. Jesus was sanctified through baptism in the sense that from this time forward, He would walk in God's purposes for Him as the Messiah and Savior of the world.

Baptism is a spiritual picture God has painted for us of how we share in Jesus' death and resurrection: *"Therefore we have been buried with Him through baptism into death, so that as Christ was raised from the dead through the glory of the Father, so we too might walk in newness of life"* (Romans 6:4).

Beginning with the first disciples and then continuing throughout the ages, water baptism has been used as a picture of sanctification, cleansing, and dedication—a setting apart of those who would follow in Christ's footsteps.

The Missing Dimensions

It's important to note that the bronze laver is one of the only pieces of tabernacle furniture for which God did not supply specific dimensions regarding its construction. When studying Exodus and Leviticus, we see that God told Moses how deep, wide, and high to make the bronze altar. He provided the size and dimensions for the table of showbread and the altar of incense. He specified the size and the dimensions for the ark of the covenant. But when it came to the specifications for the bronze laver, God was silent. Why?

Although we won't know for sure until we get to heaven, I've heard it taught—and I agree—that God could have been saying, in effect, "There are no boundaries and no limitations to My desire and My ability to wash you and set you apart. Come to Me, and I will wash you, sanctify you, and make you holy, so that you may fulfill My purpose for your life here on earth."

In a later chapter, I'm going to share with you more about how God used both Moses and Aaron to paint a spiritual picture for us of Jesus Christ. For now, I want us to note that when Moses consecrated Aaron for service in the tabernacle, God didn't say that Aaron should wash himself off, clean himself up, and sanctify himself in order to be holy enough to serve Him. No, God said that *Moses* was to wash Aaron at the bronze laver. (See Exodus 40:12.)

We need to understand that just as Aaron could not sanctify himself but needed Moses to wash him, so are we unable to sanctify ourselves through our own efforts or works. This is a picture of our need for the blood of Jesus Christ and the cleansing water of God's Word to wash and sanctify us.

Next, let's take a look at the pattern God has revealed to us through the laver being constructed from bronze mirrors.

Look in the Mirror

The bronze laver was covered with reflective mirrors because God wanted the priests to see themselves as they washed. The process of sanctification begins only when we're willing to look at ourselves in honesty and humility as we ask God to reveal the darkness of our souls.

James spoke of this "mirror" of self-examination:

For if anyone is a hearer of the word and not a doer, he is like a man who looks at his natural face in a mirror; for once he has looked at himself and gone away, he has immediately forgotten what kind of person he was. But one who looks intently at the perfect law, the law of liberty, and abides by it, not having become a forgetful hearer but an effectual doer, this man will be blessed in what he does. (James 1:23–25)

When we look into the mirror of the Word, we have a choice: We can see ourselves as God sees us and then walk away, unchanged, choosing to forget the kind of person we saw reflected there; or, we can respond to what we see by asking God to forgive our sins and to provide us with the strength and courage we need to allow Him to wash and sanctify us through His Word.

It's the Word of God that will judge us when we stand before God in heaven one day.

> [Jesus said,] *"If anyone hears My sayings and does not keep them, I do not judge him; for I did not come to judge the world, but to save the world. He who rejects Me and does not receive My sayings, has one who judges him; **the word I spoke is what will judge him at the last day.**"* (John 12:47–48)

We can come to the Word of God voluntarily and allow it to judge us while there's still time to respond to God's sanctifying process, or we can bypass His bronze laver of sanctification and let the Word judge us on the last day. Paul tells us in 1 Corinthians 11:31, *"But if we judged ourselves rightly, we would not be judged."* What a thought!

I don't know about you, but I'd rather look into the mirror of God's Word every day to see how much I need His cleansing and help. I want His Holy Scriptures to be the sword in His hand that cuts away every ungodly thing in my heart and life.

> *For the word of God is living and active and sharper than any two-edged sword, and piercing as far as the division of soul and spirit, of both joints and marrow, and able to judge the thoughts and intentions of the heart.*
> (Hebrews 4:12)

Do You Want to Go Further?

At this point in the journey, we must pause and make a choice: Do we want stay in the outer court, or are we ready to move on to the Holy Place of the inner court?

Sadly, many people choose to remain in the outer court their entire lives. Some have never moved beyond the bronze altar. They may have asked Jesus to be their Savior, but they have never developed the godly habit of repenting of their daily trespasses.

Maybe we've been water baptized, but we haven't moved any further in the sanctification process by allowing God to set us apart from the world for His purposes. We haven't chosen to come to the bronze laver with humility and honesty to peer into our reflection, repent of the sin we see there, and ask God to sanctify us with the washing of the water of the Word.

Too many of us are content with simply having our sins forgiven. We gladly accepted Jesus' blood sacrifice to atone for our sins and save us from an eternity in hell; but, since then, we've been content just to camp out in the outer court. We've become comfortable waiting for our *future* in heaven while offering the least possible amount of personal sacrifice in the *present*.

The book of Hebrews speaks of these two different stages in the Christian life. One stage is represented by those who remain babes in Christ and don't press on to maturity. The author of Hebrews said that these kinds of Christians are in danger of hardening their hearts—of coming up short and of falling away.

The other kinds of Christians are those who "hold fast," gripping firm until the end as they press on to perfection. It will be that kind of Christian who will inherit the new covenant blessings secured for us in Christ. (See Hebrews 3:4–15; 5:12–14.)

The author of Hebrews taught that we can actually be brought into God's presence by the power of Jesus' blood:

> *Therefore, brethren, since we have confidence to enter the holy place by the blood of Jesus, by a new and living way which He inaugurated for us through the veil, that is, His flesh, and since we have a great priest over the house of God, let us draw near [enter into] with a sincere heart in full assurance of faith, having our hearts sprinkled clean from an evil conscience and our bodies washed with pure water.* (Hebrews 10:19–22)

The "Hebrews" to whom that letter was addressed were most likely the early Christians in Jerusalem. Acts 21:20 lets us know that there were thousands of them. The author was writing to encourage them to *"press on to maturity"* (Hebrews 6:1) and to *"run with endurance the race that is set before [them]"* (Hebrews 12:1).

Venturing Beyond the Outer Court

Unfortunately, as in those days, there are many Christians who, after professing faith in Christ, come to a standstill. They never leave the outer court in their relationship with God. They never go beyond being acquaintances with God.

Why? Maybe it's because they don't know, or haven't been taught, that there is more for them in God. Maybe it's because they know there's more but they aren't willing to pay the price or to do what it takes to move beyond the outer court and into the inner court, moving past casual friendship and entering into a relationship of intimacy in the Holy of Holies.

Another possible reason why most Christians never venture beyond the outer court is because they have no idea what is waiting for them in the inner court and the Holy of Holies, so they look *"in a mirror"* (James 1:23) and go away, immediately forgetting who they are in Christ. Oh, my friend, if you only knew the joy, peace, union, and communion with the Father that await you in the Holy of Holies, you wouldn't waste a minute of your time; you'd run into His presence!

For whatever reason, too many Christians seem be content with the thought that their sins have been forgiven. They've come, if you will, to the bronze altar. They've accepted the sacrifice of Jesus as substitution and payment for their personal sentence of spiritual death. But they've stopped short of the inner court and the Holy of Holies. They've grown comfortable merely hoping for their future while avoiding personal sacrifice in the present, and they resist being truly "set apart" to fulfill God's purpose for their lives on earth.

In the first century, many Christians were growing cold and falling away. Some ran well for a time, only to become entangled in the affairs of the world.

In my life, I've known many Christians whose knowledge of the Word of God has outpaced their personal relationship with Him. They're excited to know more and learn more, but they end up doing less. I've found that it's possible for my mind, will, and emotions to be satisfied with knowledge, understanding, and good feelings without my heart or my spirit being attuned to what God is saying to me.

We need to be careful not to become content with our religion, our doctrine, and our Christian life, because it's possible that our hearts will become hardened. It's possible for us to live in the natural realm and find ourselves walking by sight, not by faith. When we walk by sight, we end up walking in unbelief, because our focus will be limited to the natural circumstances surrounding us.

What we see in the natural is not what God sees in the spirit. Neither is it what God wants us to see in the spirit. What God wants from us is childlike faith that lives in the invisible and in the spirit. Our faith is the ear that hears His voice.

Romans 10:10 says, *"With the heart a person believes."* That statement is true, whether you're applying it to something in the world or to something of God. It's with our heart that we believe. Unbelief takes us away from God. Faith draws us near to Him.

In the end, mere knowledge of God isn't enough. Our heart must be open to receive Him and attuned to hear what He has to say to us in that place of intimacy—in the Holy of Holies.

A great parallel for us is found in the children of Israel, who were about to enter the Promised Land. How similar we are to them in regard to our need for faith and obedience.

Digging Deeper

1. In Ephesians 5, Paul talks about being washed by the water and the Word. Are you spending regular time with God, allowing Him to wash you with the truth of His Word? If so, how are you being changed as you look into His Word? If not, what is preventing you from experiencing this cleansing process?

2. Have you ever experienced water baptism? If so, what kind of impact did this have on your walk with the Lord? If you haven't been water baptized, are you ready to be now? Why or why not?

3. Do you feel that your actions *for* God are on pace with your knowledge *of* God? Have you ever felt that you had grown too content in your relationship with God, or that your heart had become hardened? What did it take to break out of that condition—or do you *still* need to break out?

13

IT'S TIME TO GROW UP

"Therefore leaving the elementary teaching about the Christ, let us press on to maturity."
—Hebrews 6:1

When God told the children of Israel to "go up" and "possess" the land, they gave in to fear. Ten of the twelve spies came back with a negative report. It's interesting to me that all twelve of the spies saw the same giants in the land, but only two of the twelve saw God. Ten spies had their eyes stuck on the natural, while two had their eyes focused on faith and were certain of God's ability to deliver the land into their hands.

Unbelief and fear are two ingredients that cause us to be disobedient. That's why God said to them, "Because of your unbelief, because of your hardness of heart, you cannot enter in." (See Numbers 14; Psalm 95:11; Hebrews 3:11.)

These Israelites had the faith to leave Egypt, but they didn't have the faith to enter Canaan. When they were tested to see if they would *"hold fast the beginning of [their] assurance firm unto the end"* (Hebrews 3:14), they failed. They gave up.

According to the book of Hebrews, there were Christians behaving exactly the same as their forefathers had behaved in the wilderness. They had begun well, but some were now standing still, while others had even turned back.

Just like their forefathers who had left Egypt, they recognized that God had saved them from slavery; they were content with the idea of salvation through Christ as Messiah and Savior of the world, but they had no desire to press on to Canaan—to the Promised Land; to a life of sanctification, holiness, and power. They were content to camp out in the outer court.

Moses tried to encourage the children of Israel, saying, *"He brought us out from there in order to bring us in, to give us the land which He had sworn to our fathers"* (Deuteronomy 6:23). God had brought them out of Egypt so that He could bring them into the Promised Land, in the same way that Jesus brings us out of our bondage and slavery to sin in order to bring us into a deeper, more intimate, more powerful relationship with Him.

Spiritual Maturity Is a Choice

The children of Israel were glad to be brought out from the bondage and slavery of Egypt, even though they often grumbled in the wilderness. But, when faced with the choice of faith versus fear—of obedience versus disobedience; of entering the land and conquering their enemies versus continuing to wander in the wilderness—they made the wrong choice. They chose fear, disobedience, and continual wandering.

If only they had the faith to see into the invisible. If only they had the maturity to know that anything God asked them to do was for their good, to give them hope and a future, and to bless them. If only they had chosen to be obedient, they would have spared themselves great heartache.

The consequence of their unbelief and resulting disobedience was forty years of wandering—forty years of waiting for the promises of God. Aside from Joshua and Caleb, that entire generation was not allowed to "enter in," because of doubt, unbelief, fear, and disobedience. Instead, they perished in the wilderness without ever experiencing the blessings of the Promised Land firsthand.

The author of the book of Hebrews was saying, "Don't be like those disbelieving Israelites. God has so much more for you!"

The call to the inner court and to the Holy of Holies is a call to sanctification, holiness, intimacy, worship, power, and transformation. It is a call to "enter in." It's a call to take the next step and move beyond the outer court. It's a call to cease from wandering and complaining and to enter the life of victory over every enemy. It's a call to serve God in the land of promise. But we have to answer that call.

Just as there were in the first century, there are carnal Christians and there are spiritual Christians. The carnal Christians are those who have found a way, spiritually, to do something that is impossible in the natural world: remain as babies.

In the natural world, every plant, animal, and human being grows. Unless you starve someone, he is going to grow. With the proper nourishment, rest, and shelter, barring some terrible accident or debilitating sickness, a newborn baby is going to grow. I didn't say that a newborn baby will *mature*. That's a whole different discussion. But it's going to grow. Choice doesn't enter into the question of growth—in the natural realm, at least.

In the spiritual realm, many Christians have stopped growing. They have come out of Egypt, but they have remained in the wilderness of a worldly life, a life of spiritual inadequacy and immaturity, a life of living in their spiritual comfort zone of "going no farther" with Christ.

We see this type of Christian all around us. They are the ones who are content with salvation. They rest in their particular church's doctrines, teachings, and orthodoxy; its services and formalities; its spiritual political correctness. Where is the desire, hunger, and yearning for more of God, for the deeper truths of His Word, and for a deeper, more intimate relationship with Him? God has so much more for you!

In Exodus 6, God instructed Moses as to what he should tell the children of Israel. Pay attention to the five things God promised to do for His children as He was about to bring them out of Egypt. As you read, keep in mind that to most Bible scholars, Egypt represents the world's systems, beliefs, and behaviors.

Furthermore I have heard the groaning of the sons of Israel, because the Egyptians are holding them in bondage, and I have remembered My covenant. Say, therefore, to the sons of Israel, "I am the LORD, and I will bring you out from under the burdens of the Egyptians, and I will deliver you from their bondage. I will also redeem you with an outstretched arm and with great judgments. Then I will take you for My people, and I will be your God; and you shall know that I am the LORD your God, who brought you out from under the burdens of the Egyptians. I will bring you to the land which I swore to give to Abraham, Isaac, and Jacob, and I will give it to you for a possession; I am the LORD." (Exodus 6:5–8)

Let's recap:

1. *"I will bring you out from under the burdens of the Egyptians."*

2. *"I will deliver you from their bondage."*

3. *"I will also redeem you with an outstretched arm and with great judgments."*

4. *"I will take you for My people, and I will be your God; and you shall know that I am the Lord your God, who brought you out from under the burdens of the Egyptians."*

5. *"I will bring you to the land which I swore to give to Abraham, Isaac, and Jacob, and I will give it to you for a possession; I am the LORD."*

What an incredible picture of what God wants to do for His children today. God has a place and a plan of promise for you!

God's Plan in Scripture

Paul made it abundantly clear in Romans 11 that, as the church, we have been grafted into the vine of Israel and that we are partakers of God's promises and blessings to Abraham. (See also Romans 4; Galatians 3.)

God's people are to be distinct from the people of the world. The following verses map out the plans and purposes for you, as a child of God. Here are God's intentions for you, for His people:

+ *"I will set [you] apart...in order that you may know that I, the LORD, am in the midst of the land. I will put a division between My people and your people [the Egyptians; the world]"* (Exodus 8:22–23).

+ *"But the LORD will make a distinction between the livestock of Israel and the livestock of Egypt, so that nothing will die of all that belongs to the sons of Israel"* (Exodus 9:4).

+ *"For this reason I have allowed you to remain [in Egypt], in order to show you My power and in order to proclaim My name through all the earth"* (Exodus 9:16).

+ *"If you will give earnest heed to the voice of the LORD your God, and do what is right in His sight, and give ear to His commandments, and keep all His statutes, I will put none of the diseases on you which I have put on the Egyptians; for I, the LORD, am your healer"* (Exodus 15:26).

+ *"You yourselves have seen what I did to the Egyptians, and how I bore you on eagles' wings, and brought you to Myself. Now then, if you will indeed obey My voice and keep My covenant, then you shall be My own possession among all the peoples, for all the earth is Mine; and you shall be to Me a kingdom of priests and a holy nation"* (Exodus 19:4–6).

+ *"I will dwell among the sons of Israel and will be their God. They shall know that I am the LORD their God who brought them out of the land of Egypt, that I might dwell among them; I am the LORD their God"* (Exodus 29:45–46).

+ *"My presence shall go with you, and I will give you rest"* (Exodus 33:14). When we walk in obedience before God, He shows us His favor!

+ *"I am the LORD your God. Consecrate yourselves therefore, and be holy, for I am holy"* (Leviticus 11:44). God commands us to be holy.

+ *"Oh that they had such a heart in them, that they would fear Me and keep all My commandments always, that it may be well with them and with their sons forever!"* (Deuteronomy 5:29–30).

+ *"You should diligently keep the commandments of the LORD your God, and His testimonies and His statutes which He has commanded you. You shall do what is right and good in the sight of the LORD, that it may be well with you and that you may go in and possess the good land which the LORD swore to give your fathers, by driving out all your enemies from before you, as the LORD has spoken"* (Deuteronomy 6:17–19).

+ *"You are a holy people to the LORD your God; the LORD your God has chosen you to be a people for His own possession out of all the peoples who are on the face of the earth"* (Deuteronomy 7:6).

+ *"When you have eaten and are satisfied, you shall bless the LORD your God for the good land which He has given you. Beware that you do not forget the LORD your God by not keeping His commandments and His ordinances and His statutes which I am commanding you today; otherwise, when you have eaten and are satisfied, and have built good houses and lived in them, and when your herds and your flocks multiply, and your silver and gold multiply, and all that you have multiplies, then your heart will become proud and you will forget the Lord your God who brought you out from the land of Egypt, out of the house of slavery"* (Deuteronomy 8:10–14).

+ *"Now, Israel, what does the Lord your God require from you, but to fear the Lord your God, to walk in all His ways and love Him, and to serve the Lord your God with all your heart and with all your soul, and to keep the Lord's commandments and His statutes which I am commanding you today for your good?"* (Deuteronomy 10:12–13).

+ *"You are the sons of the Lord your God…you are a holy people to the Lord your God, and the Lord has chosen you to be a people for His own possession out of all the peoples who are on the face of the earth"* (Deuteronomy 14:1–2).

+ *"You have today declared the Lord to be your God, and that you would walk in His ways and keep His statutes, His commandments and His ordinances, and listen to His voice. The Lord has today declared you to be His people, a treasured possession, as He promised you, and that you should keep all His commandments; and that He will set you high above all nations which He has made, for praise, fame, and honor; and that you shall be a consecrated people to the Lord your God, as He has spoken"* (Deuteronomy 26:17–19).

If we took a journey from one end of the Bible to the other, looking for all of the places where God spoke to His children about the kind of life He wanted them to live and the kind of relationship He wanted to have with them, we would see the consequences for obedience, as well as the consequences of disobedience.

Delivered from Egypt, a Type of the World

When God delivered the Israelites from bondage in Egypt, there were two stages. First, there was the life in the wilderness, characterized by wandering, wants, needs, complaining, grumbling, unbelief, fear, and disobedience. The consequence of this behavior was the fact that God did not allow the children of Israel to "enter into" the Promised Land. They did not enter into His rest.

The second stage was living in the Promised Land. There was rest there instead of wandering. It was a land flowing with milk and honey, a land of abundance in place of lack, want, and need. It was a place of victory over every enemy instead of defeat.

Likewise, there are stages in the process of Christian growth and maturation. There are steps toward a deeper, more intimate relationship with God—to truly knowing Him.

It's one thing to know Jesus as Savior—to have come out of Egypt, so to speak. It's a completely different thing to know Him as Paul desired to know Him: To *know* Him and the power of His resurrection. (See Philippians 3:10.) It's a completely different thing to enter in and to press on to a deeper, more intimate relationship with Him in the holiness of His presence, the Holy of Holies—the fullness of communion God desires us to have with Him.

Today, may God give us the boldness, faith, and hunger to enter in and press on—to move from an outer-court relationship with Him to an inner-court relationship, and, ultimately, to the Holy of Holies.

Therefore let us draw near with confidence to the throne of grace, so that we may receive mercy and find grace to help in time of need.   (Hebrews 4:16)

Let's Grow Up

What's so wrong with the outer court? Well, as a first step, absolutely nothing. Again, spiritual maturation is a process, and God is gentle and patient with us as we grow. But He doesn't intend for us to be content with the outer-court experience. Because He loves us so much, He yearns for us to press in to access everything He has for us.

Just as He did with David, God wants to lovingly gather us into the shadow of His wings and shelter us there with His all-encompassing presence. But this kind of intimacy is possible only for those who are willing to move from the outer court to the inner court and into the Holy of Holies.

As I mentioned earlier, a baby can't remain an infant. It either grows or dies.

Here, again, we have an example of God using the natural world to teach us a spiritual truth. The book of Hebrews contains a strong exhortation for those of us who would be content to remain in the outer court, with no real desire to mature in their faith:

For though by this time you ought to be teachers, you have need again for someone to teach you the elementary principles of the oracles of God, and you have come to need milk and not solid food. For everyone who partakes only of milk is not accustomed to the word of righteousness, for he is an infant.
(Hebrews 5:12–13)

The writer seems to have been saying to the Hebrew believers, "You ought to be growing, but you're not. Why in the world are you still drinking 'outer-court milk' when you could be partaking of an 'inner-court feast' or dining at a 'Holy of Holies banquet'?"

We need to move beyond the bronze altar and the bronze laver. It's time for us to ascend the steps and enter into the inner court—the Holy Place—and to move from there into the Holy of Holies, filled with joy and anticipation and longing for what we will discover in God's presence.

Press On!

When a contractor pours a concrete foundation, he knows it is only the beginning of the building and not the building itself. In the same way, encountering the bronze altar and the bronze laver in the outer court is foundational for having a deeply intimate relationship with the Lord. But our outer-court experience is not intimacy; it merely represents an essential step on the pathway into God's presence. We must move past it if we want to have an intimate encounter with God.

Therefore leaving the elementary teaching about the Christ, let us press on to maturity, not laying again a foundation of repentance from dead works and of faith toward God, of instruction about washings and laying on of hands, and the resurrection of the dead and eternal judgment. (Hebrews 6:1–2)

While *"repentance"* and *"washings"* are foundational to our relationship with the Lord, we cannot stop there. The writer of Hebrews instructs us to move on and leave these elementary teachings behind us as we press on to spiritual maturity. We must press on if we truly desire an intimate relationship with the Lord.

The author of Hebrews compared the act of pressing in to God's presence to a race:

Therefore, since we have so great a cloud of witnesses surrounding us, let us also lay aside every encumbrance and the sin which so easily entangles us, and let us run with endurance the race that is set before us. (Hebrews 12:1)

When running a race, the runners must keep running if they want to cross the finish line and claim their prize. In the same way, we can't stop running our race until we cross the finish line and run into His arms. And, my friend, you need to know that the race doesn't end in the outer court.

I invite you to press on in this journey with me as we ascend to the inner court and then move beyond the veil into the Holy of Holies. This is where God's presence dwells, and the prize of an intimate relationship with Him is the rich reward that awaits us here. Press on!

Digging Deeper

1. How would you describe your level of spiritual maturity? Are you an infant who is content with "milk"? Are you an adolescent who is happy with "hamburger"? Or are you a spiritually mature adult who is regularly feasting on "prime rib" in the Lord's presence? Why are you at this level of spiritual maturity?

2. Reflect on times in your life when you experienced the rewards or consequences of obedience or disobedience. What did you learn about God's desire for your life? What did you learn about yourself?

3. Spend time with the Lord talking about your desire—or lack of desire—to press into a place of deeper intimacy with Him. If He reveals anything to you that is holding you back, confess it to Him, repent, and then ask for His strength and courage to run this race with endurance until you cross the finish line and leap into His waiting arms.

PART III

THE JOURNEY INWARD

14

CLIMBING THE STAIRS

"I will bless the LORD at all times; His praise shall continually be in my mouth."
—Psalm 34:1

When the Lord spoke to me that morning in the hotel coffee shop about pursuing an intimate relationship with Him, you'll recall the second word He gave me was *praise.* I knew that He was asking me to spend more time praising Him. In the months and years since then, God has gradually unfolded for me what He meant, and He has done so through the pattern of the stairs in Solomon's temple, which led from the outer court up to the inner court.

As I've dug for hidden treasure in Scripture, I've come to understand that the natural act of the priests declaring God's praises on the fifteen stairs to the temple also serves as a spiritual picture of how He calls us to praise Him faithfully as we prepare to enter into a more intimate relationship with Him.

Let's leave the outer court behind us now as we press onward and upward to access the inner court through our praises.

The Psalms of Ascent

I was poring over the book of Psalms one day when my attention was caught by the little descriptive captions at the beginning of each psalm. Some of them read "A psalm of David" or "For the choir director." But when I got to Psalm 120, I started seeing captions I didn't understand.

All fifteen captions for Psalms 120–134 are the same: "A Song of Ascents." I thought to myself, "*A Psalm of David," I understand; but what in the world is a "Psalm of Ascent"*?

So, I decided to do some gold digging.

The Hebrew word for *psalm is mizmor,* which means "a poem sung with instruments." Its root is another Hebrew word, *zamar,* which means "to touch the strings or parts of a musical instrument; to play upon; to make music accompanied by the voice; to praise." So, a psalm is a song that is sung with musical accompaniment.

I learned that after the priest had performed a sacrifice on the bronze altar and washed in the bronze laver in the outer court, he came to a set of stairs leading up to the temple, which housed the inner court and Holy of Holies. The priest would stand before the steps and sing Psalm 120.

Then, he would take the first step up and sing Psalm 121. He would take another step and sing Psalm 122, and then another step and another step, praising his way up the stairs and into the inner court.

While the wilderness tabernacle of Moses was not a place of singing, music, or dancing, Solomon's temple was quite different. I believe this is because Solomon grew up exposed to the expressive, emotional, and joyful sounds of music that his father, David, had instituted as a regular part of worship.

When David brought the ark of the covenant up to Jerusalem, the joyous processional was explosive with music:

And the children of the Levites bore the ark of God on their shoulders, by its poles, as Moses had commanded according to the word of the LORD. Then David spoke to the leaders of the Levites to appoint their brethren to be the singers accompanied by instruments of music, stringed instruments, harps, and cymbals, by raising the voice with resounding joy.

(1 Chronicles 15:15–16 NKJV)

David is credited with writing seventy-three of the psalms; in fact, according to Scripture, it was David himself who invented many of the instruments that were used: *"And 4,000 were praising the* Lord *with the instruments which David made for giving praise"* (1 Chronicles 23:5).

Even after the ark of the covenant was in place, the musical praise of God's goodness, mercy, faithfulness, and power continued because David had appointed priests to maintain ongoing worship as part of their daily responsibilities. (See 1 Chronicles 16:4–6, 37.)

It was in this rich seedbed of musical instrumentation and singing that Solomon grew until he himself was anointed as king. For him, music and singing were a normal part of worship. This is why, when Solomon dedicated the temple, he had the priests play cymbals, stringed instruments, and harps, and lift their voices in unison to praise the Lord. As they did, the glory of the Lord fell, and His presence was so strong that the priests were unable to continue ministering! (See 2 Chronicles 5:12–14.)

It's no surprise, then, that Solomon instituted the singing of psalms as a regular part of temple worship, including the Psalms of Ascent, which were sung on the steps leading up to the inner court.

Step by Step

As the priest stood before the bottom step—step 1—he would begin to sing: *"In my trouble I cried to the* Lord, *and He answered me. Deliver my soul, O* Lord, *from lying lips, from a deceitful tongue"* (Psalm 120:1–2). And then he would continue on, step by step, singing a different psalm for each of the next fourteen steps. For the sake of space, I've included only the first verse or two from each of the Psalms of Ascent, but I encourage you to read through all of them in your Bible. Just as they were an integral part of temple worship that led the priests up the stairs and into God's presence, so will the Lord use these psalms to draw you closer to Him.

Step 2:   *"I will lift up my eyes to the mountains; from where shall my help come? My help comes from the* Lord, *who made heaven and earth"* (Psalm 121:1–2).

Step 3:   *"I was glad when they said to me, 'Let us go to the house of the* Lord'" (Psalm 122:1).

Step 4:   *"To You I lift up my eyes, O You who are enthroned in the heavens!"* (Psalm 123:1).

Step 5:   *"Had it not been the* Lord *who was on our side when men rose up against us, then they would have swallowed us alive,…the waters would have engulfed us"* (Psalm 124:2–4).

Step 6:   *"Those who trust in the* Lord *are as Mount Zion, which cannot be moved but abides forever"* (Psalm 125:1).

Step 7:   *"When the* Lord *brought back the captive ones of Zion, we were like those who dream. Then our mouth was filled with laughter and our tongue with joyful shouting"* (Psalm 126:1–2).

Step 8:   *"Unless the* Lord *builds the house, they labor in vain who build it; unless the* Lord *guards the city, the watchman keeps awake in vain"* (Psalm 127:1).

Step 9:   *"How blessed is everyone who fears the* Lord, *who walks in His ways"* (Psalm 128:1).

Step 10:   *"Many times they have persecuted me from my youth up"* (Psalm 129:1).

Step 11:   *"Out of the depths I have cried to You, O* Lord. *Lord, hear my voice!"* (Psalm 130:1–2).

Step 12:   *"O* Lord, *my heart is not proud, nor my eyes haughty; nor do I involve myself in great matters, or in things too difficult for me"* (Psalm 131:1).

Step 13:   *"Remember, O* Lord, *on David's behalf, all his affliction; how he swore to the* Lord *and vowed to the Mighty One of Jacob"* (Psalm 132:1–2).

Step 14:   *"Behold, how good and how pleasant it is for brothers to dwell together in unity!"* (Psalm 133:1).

Step 15:   *"Behold, bless the* Lord, *all servants of the* Lord, *who serve by night in the house of the* Lord*!"* (Psalm 134:1).

Since God uses the natural to reveal the spiritual, let's explore the meaning of the staircase and how these fifteen psalms, incorporated into the priests' daily responsibilities, represent a treasure chest filled with gold for us to discover.

The Praise Pattern of the Stairs

The picture of a priest singing praises to God as he climbs the temple staircase to the inner court offers us a beautiful spiritual pattern of how our praise enables us to ascend from our self-absorption and earthly cares into God's presence.

In chapter 2, I shared with you how singing, shouting, playing musical instruments, clapping, and dancing are all ways to praise the Lord. Sometimes referred to as "Davidic" styles of worship because of the joyful expressions he instituted at his Jerusalem tabernacle, these can be powerful sacrifices of praise. (See Hebrews 13:15.)

Sadly, too many of us have been taught that the "correct" way to praise God is to be piously quiet. Did you know that there were many hundreds of years when music in the church was silenced altogether? In fact, after Solomon died, music, singing, and dancing also died out as expressions of temple worship. Although there were a few godly kings after him who reinstituted dynamic expressions of praise, by the time Jesus was born, musical celebration in the temple had ceased. Only the Psalms of Ascent continued as a regular use of music and song in worship.

While there is a time for us to be silent before the Lord, joyful celebration should characterize our times of praise when we're fellowshipping with other believers, as well as when we're alone in our quiet times with Him. As we discussed in chapter 2, we must be free to express our praise—spirit, soul, *and* body! Thankfully, the enemy's muzzle and chains on the body of Christ continue to be thrown off as believers around the world are learning to sing, shout, clap, and dance before the Lord with all their might!

Remember, God doesn't *need* us to praise Him. We are the ones who need to praise Him, because in doing so, we are changed. Just as the priests climbed the steps one at a time, singing God's praises, declaring Israel's desperate need for Him, and testifying of His awesome deeds and mighty acts, so must we take steps of praise every day as we acknowledge that our hope is in Him alone:

I wait for the LORD, my soul does wait, and in His word do I hope. My soul waits for the Lord more than the watchmen for the morning....O Israel, hope in the LORD; for with the LORD there is lovingkindness, and with Him is abundant redemption. (Psalm 130:5–7)

Only as we climb the staircase singing with our voices, minds, and spirits (see 1 Corinthians 14:15) will we be able to access the inner court and commune with God in the Holy of Holies. We must be priests who ascend the "steps" toward spiritual maturity with our praise, proclaiming the greatness and goodness of God.

But you are A CHOSEN RACE, A royal PRIESTHOOD, A HOLY NATION, A PEOPLE FOR GOD'S OWN POSSESSION, so that you may proclaim the excellencies of Him who has called you out of darkness into His marvelous light.

(1 Peter 2:9)

Bless the Lord

Although Paul wrote his letter to the believers in the church at Colossae more than two thousand years ago, his words are still alive with meaning for us today. He gave us this admonition: *"Let the word of Christ richly dwell within you, with all wisdom teaching and admonishing one another with psalms and hymns and spiritual songs, singing with thankfulness in your hearts to God"* (Colossians 3:16).

My friend, it's time for us to sing!

When the priest reached the fifteenth and final step before entering the inner court of the temple, he would lift up his hands and sing the final Psalm of Ascent, from Psalm 134:

Behold, bless the LORD, all servants of the LORD, who serve by night in the house of the LORD! Lift up your hands to the sanctuary and bless the LORD. May the LORD bless you from Zion, He who made heaven and earth.

(Psalm 134:1–3)

As we continue on our pathway into God's presence and prepare to enter the inner court, may we, too, lift up our hands and bless the Lord, and may He bless us with an increasingly intimate relationship with Him in return.

Digging Deeper

1. Do you find it easy to express your praise openly and joyfully to the Lord with your spirit, soul, *and* body, or is it easier to be silent before Him? Why?

2. Is praise a regular part of your personal and corporate worship times? Why or why not?

3. Read through the Psalms of Ascent. Which of these psalms best reflects your heart and the circumstances of your life right now?

4. Spend time with the Lord, praising Him for His wonderful acts. Remember, the Psalms were originally composed as songs. If you would like, pick one of the Psalms of Ascent and make up a little melody in your heart. Sing the psalm to the Lord as an expression of your love for Him. If you'd prefer not to sing, then read the psalm aloud to Him and bless His holy name.

15

FRESH OIL

"Your word is a lamp to my feet and a light to my path."
—Psalm 119:105

Do you remember the third word God gave me on that life-changing morning so long ago? After He said that I was to *repent* and *praise,* He said, *David, I want you to worship Me when you come into My presence.*

I shared with you in chapter 2 how our praise is a joy-filled expression of what God *does,* while worship expresses our love and adoration for who God *is.* Then, in the last chapter, we explored God's treasure hidden in the Psalms of Ascent and how our praise is a staircase that will lead us upward on our pathway into God's presence.

Now that we've climbed the steps of praise, I want to take the next three chapters to focus on our worship of God by mining the "gold" of the inner court. Specifically, we're going to examine the three amazing pieces of furniture contained in this holy space and discover how invaluable they are to our pursuit of intimacy with the Lord.

In the previous chapter, we looked at the temple steps leading from the outer court to the inner court. However, stairs were not part of the tabernacle in the wilderness. We're going to return to the tabernacle to see the different picture God has painted for us there..

After offering a blood sacrifice on the bronze altar and washing in the bronze laver in the outer court, the priest would pass into the inner court, which was formed by woven linen curtains and measured 300 square feet. It contained only three pieces of furniture: the gold lampstand, the table of showbread, and the altar of incense.

Moses had each of these pieces constructed according to the pattern God had given him on the mountain, and each piece has incredible meaning for those of us seeking the pathway into God's presence. First, let's take a closer look at the gold lampstand. (See Reference figure A-2.)

The Gold Lampstand

In the outer court, the sun shone brightly by day and the moon by night. But when the priest stepped into the inner court, his eyes had to adjust to the near darkness, which was broken only by the light shining from the gold lampstand on his left. A description of this piece of furniture is provided in Exodus:

Then you shall make a lampstand of pure gold. The lampstand and its base and its shaft are to be made of hammered work; its cups, its bulbs and its flowers shall be of one piece with it. Six branches shall go out from its sides; three branches of the lampstand from its one side and three branches of the lampstand from its other side. Three cups shall be shaped like almond blossoms in the one branch, a bulb and a flower, and three cups shaped like almond blossoms in the other branch, a bulb and a flower—so for six branches going out from the lampstand; and in the lampstand four cups shaped like almond blossoms, its bulbs and its flowers. A bulb shall be under the first pair of branches coming out of it, and a bulb under the second pair of branches coming out of it, and a bulb under the third pair of branches coming out of it, for the six branches coming out of the lampstand. Their bulbs and their branches shall be of one piece with it; all of it shall be one piece of hammered work of pure gold. Then you shall make its lamps seven in number; and they shall mount its lamps so as to shed light on the space in front of it. Its snuffers and their trays shall be of pure gold. It shall be made from a talent of pure gold, with all these utensils. See that you make them after the pattern for them, which was shown to you on the mountain. (Exodus 25:31–40)

The entire lampstand was hammered from a single piece of pure gold, with a large center branch that had three branches to the left and three branches to the right, for a total of seven branches.

As I mentioned before, numbers are important to God, and He uses them to reveal spiritual truths. The number *seven* is significant throughout the Bible, and it indicates perfection. John wrote seven messages to seven churches. (See Revelation 2–3.) Revelation 5:6 and Isaiah 11:2 speak of the seven spirits of God. There are seven continents on planet Earth. And there were seven branches on the lampstand.

Like the bronze laver in the outer court, God didn't mandate specific measurements for the lampstand. However, He was very specific about what was to be molded onto each of the six branches:

+ three cups for holding the oil and wicks
+ three almond buds
+ three almond flowers

It's important to note that there were a total of nine items molded into *each* of the six side branches. The center branch had four sets of cups, almond buds, and almond flowers, for a total of twelve molded pieces. We'll come back to this in just a minute.

A Priestly Job

In addition to opening and closing the temple gates, offering the daily sacrifices, and cleaning the previous day's ashes from the bronze altar, the priests also had daily responsibilities within the inner court, one of which was attending to the gold lampstand. God told Moses what the priests' basic duties were to include for this significant piece of furniture:

Command the sons of Israel that they bring to you clear oil from beaten olives for the light, to make a lamp burn continually....Aaron shall keep it in order from evening to morning before the LORD *continually; it shall be a perpetual statute throughout your generations. He shall keep the lamps in order on the pure gold lampstand before the* LORD *continually.*   (Leviticus 24:2–4)

Every morning and every evening, a priest would enter the inner court, bringing with him a flask of pure olive oil, a pair of scissors, and a pan filled with burning coals from the bronze altar and new wicks made from the used garments of the priests. Once inside, he would carefully inspect the lampstand to see if he needed to...

- refill any of the cups that might have run out of oil.

- trim any hardened wicks that couldn't draw up the oil. (Note: The pieces of trimmed wicks would be taken outside the camp later and buried.)

- put new wicks in the lamps that needed them.

- relight any wicks that had burned out, using coal from the bronze altar in the outer court.

Why was the gold lampstand so important to God, and why is it significant for us today? Let's dig for the buried treasure hidden in the Word.

"Thy Word Is a Lamp"

As I've already mentioned, according to Exodus 25:31–40, there were a total of nine items molded into *each* of the six side branches. The center branch had a total of twelve molded pieces.

If we add together all the cups, almond buds, and flowers in the three branches to the left of the center branch, there are 27 molded pieces ($9 \times 3 = 27$). If we add 27 to the 12 molded pieces of the center branch, it totals 39 molded pieces ($27 + 12 = 39$). Do you know how many books are in the Old Testament? Thirty-nine!

Next, if we count the number of all the cups, buds, and flowers in the three branches to the right of the center branch, again, we get the number 27. How many books are in the New Testament? Twenty-seven!

Adding these two numbers together, we get 66—the number of books in the Bible. So if we add together all of the cups, buds, and flowers on all of the lampstand branches, we get 66 (39 + 27 = 66). How many books are in the entire Bible? **66!** Amazing! There were 66 cups, bulbs, and flowers in the gold lampstand, and there are 66 books in the Bible!

Since we know God uses the natural to reveal the spiritual, we must ask what He is saying to us in the pattern of the gold lampstand. What's the significance? The Word of God is our source of illumination!

To those who want to read only the New Testament, or for those who prefer to study the Old Testament alone, I say, "You can't focus exclusively on the thirty-nine books of the Old Testament or the twenty-seven books of the New Testament. It takes the entire sixty-six books of the Bible to illuminate the full revelation of God's Word!"

While hundreds of religious manuscripts were written in the first centuries of the early church, only sixty-six of these were chosen by the church fathers to be canonized as God's Word. I've heard scholars refer to the "lost books" of the Bible, such as the Gospel of Judas or the Gospel According to Thomas. They argue that certain Gnostic Gospels should have been included but were deliberately left out of Scripture.

However, when we discover the pattern of God's Word hidden in the gold lampstand, it's evident that God's Holy Spirit supernaturally guided those responsible for deciding what to include and what to exclude from the Bible in their selection. God Himself chose the number of books destined to be included in His Holy Word long before the Torah was ever recorded, the Old Testament written, or the Old and New Testaments compiled and canonized.

When we understand that one of God's significant patterns reflected in the gold lampstand is the illuminating power of His Word, this Scripture verse takes on a whole new meaning: *"Your word is a lamp to my feet and a light to my path"* (Psalm 119:105).

When we need direction, God's Word is a lamp to show us the way. When we need encouragement, God's Word is a light of hope. When we need to repent, God's Word shines in our darkness. When we need wisdom, God's Word illumines our path. When we need to be reminded of His love, God's Word is a flame of reassurance.

The Light of the World

The gold lampstand was the only source of light in the otherwise darkened inner court. In the same way, Jesus Christ is the only true source of Light in a sin-darkened world. Jesus said, *"I am the Light of the world; he who follows Me will not walk in the darkness, but will have the Light of life"* (John 8:12). And to His disciples—including us today—Jesus says, *"You are the light of the world. A city set on a hill cannot be hidden; nor does anyone light a lamp and put it under a basket, but on the lampstand, and it gives light to all who are in the house"* (Matthew 5:14–15). Just as the brightly burning gold lampstand that enabled the priest to see in the inner court, we as believers are called to be a city set on a hill, shining brightly for the lost and those seeking to see their way to God.

The olive oil that fueled the lampstand represents the illumination, presence, power, and glory of the Holy Spirit, from whom we draw our "fuel" to provide light for others.

Those lost in darkness will be drawn to the Light of Jesus shining within us, as long as we allow Him to burn brightly in our life. In order for this to happen, we must increasingly be conformed to the image of Jesus, a transformation that necessitates changing our very thought process. Paul said, *"Let this mind be in you which also was in Christ Jesus"* (Philippians 2:5 NKJV). We're to have the mind of Christ. We're to think His thoughts.

The lampstand was made from beaten gold, which speaks of workmanship and the process of molding and forming the metal. In the same way, God wants to mold and shape our hearts and minds so that we become conformed to the image of His Son. The illumination of our minds depends on the degree to which we choose to yield and submit our will to God's.

The process of conforming our thought life to the mind of Christ is not something we are capable of doing on our own. We must depend on the Holy Spirit for power and strength to change. It is not easy or automatic, but God has used the natural picture of the lampstand's wicks to show what He expects and to prove that it is possible for us to be a *"city set on a hill"*—a light to a dark and dying world.

Trimming Our Wicks

Twice every day, the priest entered the inner court to trim any hardened or clogged wicks, because untrimmed, hard, or clogged wicks won't burn. What pattern is God revealing to us through this practice?

Each one of us is a priest called to offer spiritual sacrifices to God (see 1 Peter 2:5), and our body is the Holy Spirit's temple (see 1 Corinthians 6:19). One of our daily responsibilities is to visit the "inner court" of our lives—the place where our mind, will, and emotions dwell—and stand before the spiritual lampstand—Jesus Christ and the illuminating power of God's Word—to trim our wicks and make sure our lamps are still burning brightly for Him.

In chapter 8, we talked about the vital necessity of guarding our "gates" from the unholy things we've allowed to access our personal temple. These same sins also "clog our wicks" and block the oil of the Holy Spirit's anointing and power. There are times when we want to come into the inner court and draw near to God's presence, but we can't, because our wick has become clogged and the fire has gone out.

How do we light the fire again? We ask God to pour the oil of His Holy Spirit over us again. We act as the priests of our temple and trim the wick, cutting away any part of our heart that has become hardened through sin or neglect. We confess our sins to God, ask for forgiveness, and then relight our flame from the coals of the bronze altar of repentance.

A Personal Responsibility

Just as the tabernacle priests had to check the cups for oil, trim the hardened wicks, and relight the flame, I am responsible for maintaining my lampstand. If I somehow run out of oil—the presence of the Holy Spirit—I must ask God to replenish it.

I can't expect Him to say, "David, you're looking a little dry, Son. Let Me fill you up." This is not the pattern He has given us in Scripture. God didn't supernaturally refill the bowls of the gold lampstand with oil, and He's not going to automatically fill me with His Holy Spirit when I've run dry. Yes, He *will* fill me up, but it's *my* responsibility to come to Him in humility and ask.

It wasn't God's job to trim the hardened wicks of the gold lampstand. He didn't reach down from heaven with giant scissors and say, "Here, let Me just trim this up." It was the priest's job. And it's not God's job to reach down and automatically cut the sin from our lives. It's our responsibility to respond, when His Holy Spirit convicts us of sin, by repenting before God and trusting in the sacrificial blood of Jesus Christ from the bronze altar to cover our sin.

God didn't grab a coal off the altar in the outer court and relight the lampstand's extinguished wicks; the priest was required to do this. And if we want to have the flame of our extinguished wicks reignited, we must go to the altar, confess our daily trespasses, and allow the coals from the fire that never dies to light our wick again.

Beware of "Wick-Cloggers"

What are some of the things that can cause our wick to become clogged or hardened and eventually burn out?

+ The cares of this world
+ Overcrowded, busy schedules
+ Our own sin
+ Sickness
+ Marital problems
+ Rebellious children
+ Financial crises
+ The loss of a loved one
+ Shame from past mistakes
+ Bitterness and unforgiveness
+ Disappointment in God, ourselves, or others
+ And so on

Regardless of why we have run out of the Holy Spirit's oil, it's time for us to come to God and ask Him for the fresh oil of His Holy Spirit. It's time to cut away the dead wicks in our life that have become clogged and to get rid of the things that are causing our heart to become hardened against the Lord. It's time to go to the altar of repentance and receive fresh fire. As we do, we will be prepared to truly worship the Lord, to move beyond praising Him for what He's done and is doing, and progress into heartfelt expressions of awe and worship for who He is.

We've traveled far on the pathway to God's presence, from the gates to the bronze altar to the stairs leading to the inner court and into the inner court, where the golden lampstand illuminates our steps, fueled by the oil of the Holy Spirit.

In this place, we receive a deepening sense of His presence and a taste of the intimacy that awaits us in the Holy of Holies. But we haven't arrived yet. There are still two more pieces of furniture for us to examine in the inner court—two more spiritual pictures to consider; two more buried treasures for which we must dig.

Come with me to examine the table of showbread. Let's worship the Lord together!

Digging Deeper

1. Go back and review the list of things that can clog our "wicks." Which ones apply to you? As the priest of your temple, how will you "trim your wick"?

2. The oil of the gold lampstand represents the oil of the Holy Spirit. In what areas of your life do you need to receive fresh oil from Him?

3. In order to relight an extinguished flame, the priest used a burning coal from the bronze altar of repentance. Is there persistent sin in your life that has caused the fire of your wick to burn out?

4. Spend time with the Lord. Invite Him to show you what is clogging your wick, and then repent of it. Read His Word to illuminate any dark areas in your life. Pray for the Holy Spirit to be poured out like fresh oil and for His holy flame to be reignited in your heart.

16

DAILY BREAD

"I am the bread of life."
—John 6:48

Another name for the inner court of the tabernacle was the "Holy Place." The Hebrew word for *holy* is *qadosh*, which means "set apart; dedicated to sacred purposes." While the Israelites could access the outer court of the tabernacle, only those priests who were ceremonially clean could come into the inner court, which God had set apart as a holy and sacred place meant for worshipping Him.

In this place of worship, let's examine the pattern in the second of the three pieces of furniture contained in the inner court: the table of showbread. (See Reference figure B-1.) Another name used in Scripture for "showbread" was the *"bread of the Presence."* (For example, see Exodus 25:30.) Clearly the Lord was in this holy place. What is His pattern saying to us?

The Table of Showbread

As the priest entered the inner court, the table of showbread was on his right, immediately across from the gold lampstand, which would have cast its light over the table. The following passage from Exodus 25 provides us with a description of this fascinating piece of furniture:

> You shall make a table of acacia wood, two cubits long and one cubit wide and one and a half cubits high. You shall overlay it with pure gold and make a gold border around it. You shall make for it a rim of a handbreadth around it; and you shall make a gold border for the rim around it. You shall make four gold rings for it and put rings on the four corners which are on its four feet. The rings shall be close to the rim as holders for the poles to carry the table. You shall make the poles of acacia wood and overlay them with gold, so that with them the table may be carried. You shall make its dishes and its pans and its jars and its bowls with which to pour drink offerings; you shall make them of pure gold. You shall set the bread of the Presence on the table before Me at all times.
> (Exodus 25:23–30)

According to these specifications, the table of showbread was fairly small—only about three feet long, one-and-a-half feet deep, and two-and-a-half feet high. However, because it was made of acacia wood and overlaid with gold, it was heavy, probably weighing several hundred pounds.

The priests were responsible for baking the bread that sat on the table. (See 1 Chronicles 9:32; 23:29.) They used the finest wheat flour to make twelve large, round loaves of bread, which were replaced every Sabbath. According to God's directions, the bread was placed on the table in two stacks that sat side by side, with six loaves in each stack. There were also bowls of frankincense on the table. (See Leviticus 24:5–9.)

When they brought in the fresh showbread, the attending priests were to consume the previous week's bread while still in the holy place. Rabbinical tradition says that even though it had sat for a week, when the priests ate the showbread, it was still as warm and fresh as when they had first set it out.

The spiritual pattern of the showbread is so heavy with meaning for us today that we don't have to dig very deep to find the treasure God has hidden for us in these fragrant loaves.

The Bread of Our Will

I believe one of the things bread symbolizes in Scripture is the strength of our will.

+ *"By the sweat of your face you will eat **bread,** till you return to the ground"* (Genesis 3:19). Only through striving and strength of will would Adam and Eve have bread to eat.

+ *"So now also, please listen to the voice of your maidservant, and let me set a piece of **bread** before you that you may eat and have **strength** when you go on your way"* (1 Samuel 28:22). Eating bread provided both physical strength and endurance of will to go on.

+ *"He causes…wine that makes glad the heart of man, oil to make his face shine, and **bread** which **strengthens** man's heart"* (Psalm 104:14–15 NKJV). Bread brings strength to the heart, which speaks of our emotions and our *will.*

I want to offer you eight truths I believe God has revealed through the pattern of the showbread, as it relates to our will.

Truth #1: The showbread was in the Lord's presence twenty-four hours a day. In the same way, we must make sure our will is aligned with God's will by setting it before Him 24/7 for His inspection.

Truth #2: The showbread was made of the finest wheat flour, which, according to rabbinical tradition, was ground by being passed through eleven sieves. Likewise, our will is acceptable to God only when it is has been "ground" and refined as much as that flour.

Truth #3: Each loaf of showbread had to be molded, just as our will must be molded to God's will.

Truth #4: After the bread was molded, it was baked in a hot oven. Heat represents testing. We mustn't think it strange when we go through fiery ordeals; this is simply the "bread" of our will being tested and purified.

Truth #5: The showbread was put on the table in an ordered structure ordained by God. We, too, must allow our lives to be ordered and structured by God. Without His discipline, we can't be true disciples.

Truth #6: The bread was surrounded by frankincense. In Scripture, frankincense represents worship. Our strength to do the will of God comes in large part through our worship of Him.

Truth #7: Because the showbread was precious, there was a protective rim built into the table to prevent crumbs from falling to the ground. The protection of our will is found in Luke 21:36: "**Watch** *therefore, and* **pray** *always*" (NKJV). Our will is protected when we watch and pray.

Truth #8: The showbread was replaced with fresh loaves on a weekly basis. This speaks of our need to regularly rededicate our will to God. Like Jesus, we must not seek to do our own will, but rather *"the will of Him who sent* [Jesus]" (John 5:30).

Fresh Manna

The showbread is also a spiritual picture of the Word of God.

God required the priests to regularly supply fresh bread for the Holy Place, as a picture of the manna He supplied for the children of Israel, to sustain, strengthen, and nourish them in the wilderness. Without it, they would have died. Every morning, the Israelites would go out and gather the manna needed for that day. If they tried to collect enough for the next day, it *"bred worms and became foul"* (Exodus 16:20).

Remember, God uses the natural to reveal the spiritual. What is the pattern He wants us to see in the manna? It is this: We depend on Him for our daily bread. We must go to Him every day to receive spiritual nourishment from His Word—nourishment that will sustain and strengthen us to do all that He calls us to do.

We can't just "eat the Word" at church on Sunday and expect it provide all the spiritual strength we'll need for the coming week. No, like the Israelites in the wilderness, we must gather what we need from the Lord each day. Sadly, many believers go days, weeks, months, and even years without seeking spiritual strength from His Word.

In the natural, if we tried going that long without a meal, what would happen? *We would die.* And, believe me, it wouldn't take months or years. If we didn't eat, most of us would probably be dead within forty or fifty days. We *must* eat to live—not once a week, not once a month, but *every day*. There are serious health consequences when we choose to stop eating or neglect our bodies by giving them a steady diet of junk food.

God placed the natural law of self-preservation in the world. You have to eat to live. You don't need to believe the law, but if you break the law, you will pay the price. There are always consequences to disobedience.

In the same way, for us to be spiritually alive and healthy, we must eat daily from the table of the Lord and feast on His life-sustaining Word. Anything less leaves us weak and malnourished, and makes our spiritual immune system vulnerable to attack. When we're feeling spiritually weak, fearful, tempted, or distracted by ungodly thoughts, we need to consider that we may be spiritually malnourished. If so, all we need to do is start feasting regularly on the Word of God!

Once again, God is using the natural to reveal the spiritual. Spiritual nourishment comes from "eating" the Word.

Our Daily Bread

When Jesus was tempted by Satan in the wilderness to turn stones into bread, He responded by quoting from Deuteronomy 8:3, which says:

He humbled you and let you be hungry, and fed you with manna which you did not know, nor did your fathers know, that He might make you understand that man does not live by bread alone, but man lives by everything that proceeds out of the mouth of the LORD.

Even though Jesus was physically weak because of His forty-day fast, He was able to overcome the enemy's temptations because He was spiritually strong from eating the bread of God's Word. (See Matthew 4:4; Luke 4:4.)

When the disciples asked Jesus to teach them to pray, one of the things He taught them to ask the Father was, *"Give us each day our daily bread"* (Luke 11:3). Was He talking about physical bread? Yes! Was He talking about spiritual bread? Yes!

Scripture says that Jesus spent time with God in the morning (see Mark 1:35) and in the evening (see Matthew 14:23). David, too, prayed in the morning (see Psalm 59:16) and in the evening (see Psalm 141:2). Personally, I prefer to spend time with the Lord and to read my Bible in the morning. Once my day gets started, I'm going in fifty different directions, and there's just no getting it back, so if I want to "eat" the Word, I have to get up early and spend time with the Lord.

However, the time of day we choose to spend with God to receive nourishment and strength from Him and His Word isn't as important as our just *doing* it.

The Bread of Heaven

The showbread also reveals the pattern of Jesus as our Bread of heaven.

In John 6, remembering that Jesus had miraculously multiplied fishes and loaves to feed five thousand, the people demanded another sign that He truly was sent from God. They brought up the manna from heaven, which God had provided for their ancestors in the wilderness, perhaps with the hope that Jesus would perform a similar miracle that day. However, He responded by telling them,

> *Truly, truly, I say to you, it is not Moses who has given you the bread out of heaven, but it is My Father who gives you the true bread out of heaven. For the bread of God is that which comes down out of heaven, and gives life to the world....I am the bread of life. Your fathers ate the manna in the wilderness, and they died. This is the bread which comes down out of heaven, so that one may eat of it and not die. I am the living bread that came down out of heaven; if anyone eats of this bread, he will live forever; and the bread also which I will give for the life of the world is My flesh.* (John 6:32–33; 48–51)

Jesus was trying to show them the pattern: "*I* am the manna! *I* am the showbread!" But they couldn't understand the spiritual because they were too preoccupied with the natural.

As the disciples celebrated the last Passover meal they would share with Jesus on earth, He provided them with a powerful spiritual picture. He broke the bread, blessed it, and said, "*Take, eat; this is My body*" (Matthew 26:26). In Scripture, leaven represents sin; just as the Passover bread had no leaven in it, so Jesus had no sin in Him. The disciples must have been stunned when they realized that Jesus was telling them that the unleavened bread they were eating in the natural symbolized Him as their spiritual bread.

In the church's ancient Communion liturgy, when it's time to eat the bread, the minister says, "Feed on Him in your heart, by faith, with thanksgiving." Every time we observe Communion, we acknowledge that the bread we eat symbolizes Jesus' body, which was broken for us on the cross. By observing the sacrament of Communion, we are obeying His commandment to remember Him (see Luke 22:19), and, as we do, we're recommitting ourselves to Him, as our Savior and Lord.

Just as Jesus invited His disciples to "take and eat," He invites us to do the same. To "take and eat" means...

+ to choose to submit the strength of your will to God's will.

+ to consume the bread of God's Word on a daily basis.

+ to feed on Jesus Christ, your manna sent from God.

When we receive Jesus as our Bread, we will find our spirit growing increasingly strong, healthy, and nourished; and, like Jesus, we will be able to overcome the temptations of the evil one.

In the inner court, we've examined the gold lampstand and the table of showbread and discovered how these two items together form a powerful picture and pattern of the Light of the Word and the Light of Christ, the Bread of the Word, and the Bread of heaven. But there is still one more vital piece of furniture for us to study in the inner court before we can continue on the pathway into the intimacy of God's presence and move beyond the veil into the Holy of Holies.

Digging Deeper

1. Would you describe yourself as a strong-willed person? In what ways have you conformed your will to God's will? What areas of your life do you still need to submit to Him?

2. How often are you "eating" the Word of God? Daily? Weekly? Monthly? Only on Sundays? Never? How have your daily "eating habits" impacted your walk with the Lord and the intimacy of your relationship with Him?

3. *Communion* is a word formed by combing two words: *common* and *union*. Would you describe your relationship with the Lord as being a "common union"? Why or why not?

4. Spend time with the Lord. Tell Him how your heart yearns to be intimate with Him. Confess any areas of your life that you're afraid or unwilling

to submit to His will, and cry out for His courage, grace, and strength to help you. Ask God to show you where, how, and when He wants you to feed on His Word on a daily basis, and then joyfully begin to feast!

17

A SWEET-SMELLING SACRIFICE

*"May my prayer be counted as incense before You; the lifting up of my hands
as the evening offering."*
—Psalm 141:2

While the outer court was a place of noise and activity, the inner court was a place of quiet and stillness. Apart from the few responsibilities the priest needed to attend to, there wasn't much to do. Busyness wasn't an issue in the inner court.

Here, the priest's spirit could more easily be at rest. Here, he could kneel quietly in reverential awe before the Most High. Here, he could almost hear the prophet's words: *"The LORD is in His holy temple. Let all the earth be silent before Him"* (Habakkuk 2:20).

The inner court was a place for worship—but not for joyous celebration with singing, clapping, and dancing. Rather, the inner court was a place of silence, which, in itself, can be a form of worship. Even heaven is sometimes a place of silent worship:

When the Lamb broke the seventh seal, there was silence in heaven for about half an hour. And I saw the seven angels who stand before God, and seven trumpets were given to them. Another angel came and stood at the altar, holding a golden censer; and much incense was given to him, so that he might add it to the prayers of all the saints on the golden altar which was before the throne. And the smoke of the incense, with the prayers of the saints, went up before God out of the angel's hand. (Revelation 8:1–4)

From this passage, we discover that there is a golden altar and *"much incense"* in heaven's temple. We also know from Exodus 30 that there was a golden altar and incense in the inner court of the earthly tabernacle. (See Reference figure B-2.) Since heaven is where God gave Moses the pattern for building the wilderness tabernacle, it makes perfect sense that there would be a golden altar and incense in the Holy Place, as well.

And it's to this golden altar and the incense of the inner court that we now turn our attention.

The Altar of Incense

When the priest entered the inner court of the tabernacle, the gold lampstand was to his left; the golden table of showbread was to his right, directly across from the lampstand; and the golden altar of incense was straight ahead, in front of the veil separating the inner court from the Holy of Holies.

In Exodus 30:1–10, God provided Moses with detailed instructions regarding the building of the golden altar. The altar of incense…

+ was made of acacia wood and overlaid with gold.
+ formed a perfect square of one-and-a-half feet by one-and-a-half feet and was three feet tall (one cubit by one cubit by one-and-a-half cubits).
+ had a crown molding around the top edge.
+ had a horn on each of the four corners of the top edge.
+ had gold rings and acacia poles overlaid with gold for transporting it.

The priest would fill a pan with coals taken from the bronze altar in the outer court and bring it into the inner court in order to relight any extinguished wicks on the gold lampstand, and then he would add more coals to the ones already burning on the altar of incense. Every morning and every evening, while the sin offerings were being sacrificed in the outer court, the priest added more coals and incense to the altar in the inner court.

As with the fire on the bronze altar, the fire on the golden altar of the inner court was never allowed to burn out. Incense was to arise continually before God day and night. Historians report that those who were downwind from the Israelite camp could smell the fragrance of the incense from miles away, which indicates just how much incense burned on this altar night and day.

Once a year, on the Day of Atonement, the high priest atoned for the sins of the people by taking blood from the sin offering sacrificed on the bronze altar in the outer court and putting it on each of the horns on the four corners of the altar of incense. This was the only sign of sacrifice made on this inner court altar; burnt offerings, grain offerings, and drink offerings were reserved for the outer court altar alone. The only thing to be offered on the altar of incense was incense.

God also provided detailed instructions for the ingredients of the incense burned on the golden altar.

Incense Ingredients

God gave Moses detailed instructions on how to prepare the incense:

Take for yourself spices, stacte and onycha and galbanum, spices with pure frankincense; there shall be an equal part of each. With it you shall make incense, a perfume, the work of a perfumer, salted, pure, and holy. You shall beat some of it very fine, and put part of it before the testimony in the tent of meeting where I will meet with you; it shall be most holy to you. The incense which you shall make, you shall not make in the same proportions for yourselves; it shall be holy to you for the LORD. (Exodus 30:34–37)

On the Day of Atonement, in addition to anointing the horns of the gold altar with blood from the outer court sacrifice, the high priest would take coals from the altar of incense and handfuls of incense into the Holy of Holies, so that a cloud of incense would cover God's mercy seat. Doing so prevented the priest's death. (See Leviticus 16:12–13.)

As with the other pieces of furniture in the inner court, the golden altar and the incense it held are full of buried treasure. Let's dig for the pattern and discover the mysteries God has provided with this powerful picture.

Pursuing the Pattern

The incense on the altar represents the worship we offer up to God. Just as the altar's incense was to rise continuously before Him, so are our prayers to arise unceasingly to the Lord.

May my prayer be counted as incense before You; the lifting up of my hands as the evening offering. (Psalm 141:2)

Pray without ceasing. (1 Thessalonians 5:17)

Evening and morning and at noon I will pray, and cry aloud, and He shall hear my voice. (Psalm 55:17 NKJV)

The Israelites trusted that God would hear and respond to the prayers offered on their behalf by the priest in this holy place. In fact, it was at the altar of incense in Solomon's temple where one of their priests—Zacharias, father of John the Baptist—had a dramatic spiritual encounter, testifying that God considered the gold altar to be a significant place of prayer indeed.

Serving as a priest in the inner court was a rare honor, and those who were privileged to fulfill these duties were decided by the drawing of lots. Because Zacharias was not a high priest, this may very well have been his only opportunity to be close to God's presence and pray before the altar of incense. As Zacharias was performing his priestly duties by adding incense to the altar and interceding for the people, he also could have been praying fervently for God to miraculously intervene by ending the barrenness he and his wife, Elizabeth, had suffered for many years.

The angel Gabriel suddenly appeared to Zacharias beside the altar of incense and prophesied the birth of a son, who would eventually be known in Scripture and throughout the ages as John the Baptist. The first words Gabriel said were, *"Do not be afraid, Zacharias, for **your petition has been heard**"* (Luke 1:13).

We, too, can trust that as we go to the altar of incense within the inner court of our personal temple and minister there as priests before God, our prayers and intercessions arise to Him. He hears and responds to the prayers of those who love Him and who cry out for His mercy and intervention in the midst of their need; those who pray, like David, something like this:.

> O God, hasten to deliver me; O LORD, hasten to my help! Let those be ashamed and humiliated who seek my life; let those be turned back and dishonored who delight in my hurt. Let those be turned back because of their shame who say, "Aha, aha!" Let all who seek You rejoice and be glad in You; and let those who love Your salvation say continually, "Let God be magnified." But I am afflicted and needy; hasten to me, O God! You are my help and my deliverer; O LORD, do not delay. (Psalm 70:1–5)

Like David, cry out to God "evening and morning and at noon" (Psalm 55:17 NKJV), and trust that He is your Help and your Deliverer who will come to your aid.

A Recipe for Intercession

There is a fascinating story in Numbers 16 about the incense from the gold altar and the impact it had as a symbol of intercession. The people had turned against Moses and Aaron. Because of their murmuring and accusation, God had sent a plague to destroy them. He warned Moses and Aaron to get away from the people in order to protect themselves, but the two men responded by falling on their faces before Him.

Then, instead of running away from the people, Moses told Aaron to go quickly and get fire and incense from the altar and then run to the people. Aaron immediately obeyed, and as he ran into their midst with the incense, the plague stopped. What stopped the plague? The incense. Clearly, God considered this to be powerful stuff!

For many years, I read again and again the recipe given in Exodus 30 for the incense used on the golden altar, and I must confess that I never really understood its importance.

Then the LORD said to Moses, "Take for yourself spices, stacte and onycha and galbanum, spices with pure frankincense; there shall be an equal part of each. With it you shall make incense, a perfume, the work of a perfumer, salted, pure, and holy." (Exodus 30:34–35)

However, my understanding changed the day my good friend and Bible scholar Dick Reuben explained to me that each of the five ingredients had special significance. I now realize that, through these spices, God had hidden yet another marvelous pattern in His Word from which we can learn in order to grow in intimacy with Him.

Although later rabbinical teachings list eleven—or even thirteen—different spices, we are going to limit our study to the five ingredients listed in Exodus 30.

Stacte

Stacte is a resin that oozes freely out of the myrrh tree (like sap from a pine tree). Harvesters could come along and simply scrape it off. They didn't have to drill into the tree to reach the sap; it just came out naturally.

What's the pattern?

God desires that our worship and prayers flow from us freely. He doesn't want to force us to adore Him or communicate with Him. He doesn't want a pastor or a teacher to make us honor Him or intercede before Him. God desires our love for Him to be so great and so overwhelming that worship and prayer "ooze" out of us spontaneously. He wants it to be so "natural" for us to praise and worship Him that it feels unnatural if we don't.

Onycha

Onycha comes from a shellfish found deep in the Red Sea. When properly prepared, onycha enhances the other ingredients in an incense mixture.

What's the pattern?

God wants our worship and prayers to come from the very depths of our heart. The psalmist said,

*Deep calls to deep at the sound of Your waterfalls; all Your breakers and Your waves have rolled over me. The L*ORD *will command His lovingkindness in the daytime; and His song will be with me in the night, a prayer to the God of my life.* (Psalm 42:7–8)

As we intercede before God, aided by the Holy Spirit's *"deep groanings"* (Romans 8:26), His lovingkindness will wash over us.

Galbanum

Galbanum is a plant from the family of umbelliferae, originating in Persia and common in the Amanus regions of Syria. When a branch is broken, it spontaneously produces a milky juice, which, when dried, takes the form of a pale, waxy, yellow-green gum resin.

What's the pattern?

The significance in this pattern, as it relates to our prayers and worship, is the word *spontaneously*. Too often, we allow the painful circumstances of life to cause us to turn away from God in anger and bitterness. But His heart's desire is for us to bring Him our brokenness and surrender it to Him. It's from those broken places that the sweet incense of Christ can arise as a sacrifice of praise.

Pure Frankincense

Frankincense, sometimes called olibanum, is an aromatic resin. It also comes from a split in a branch and is tapped from a slash in a Boswellia tree. Unlike galbanum, which begins oozing from the cut right away, frankincense takes many hours to make its way to the surface of the tree—a process that happens only in the early morning hours. Tapping is done two to three times a year, with the final tap producing the purest form and most intense aroma.

What's the pattern?

Although our human nature is to avoid wounds and sorrows, it is this very process that produces the finest of incense. When, like Job, we can say, *"Though He slay me, yet will I trust Him"* (Job 13:15 NKJV), our worship is as pure incense to Him. When everything is still and quiet and we're alone with Him, He will minister His comfort and love to us, and we can minister our trust and love to Him, in return.

Salt

Salt has been recognized throughout the centuries as a flavor enhancer, purifier, and preservative.

What's the pattern?

God has called us to be the salt of the earth. (See Matthew 5:13.) As we live out our lives in faithfulness before God and others, and as our worship and prayers arise to Him from the altar of incense within us, He will use us to "salt" those around us.

A Fine Beating

God instructed Moses to take the stacte, onycha, galbanum, frankincense, and salt and *"beat some of it very fine"* (Exodus 30:36). This means that once the resins had dried, they needed to be ground into a fine powder, through a crushing process that required the perfumer to exert heavy pressure using a mortar and pestle as grinding tools. The perfumer would grind the four ingredients individually until they had been pulverized to a fine dust. He would then mix them together with salt and allow the mixture to age, so that the various aromas could blend and intensify.

Most of us have experienced circumstances in life in which we have felt like we're in a mortar, being ground and ground by God, the divine Perfumer, until we've been reduced to a powder, and all we want is for the pressure to let up and the crushing to stop.

When we're walking through a season such as this, it's easy to question if God truly loves us. His compassion seems distant and His mercy nonexistent. But this is not true. God's love for us never ends. His compassion never fails. His mercy is new every morning. His faithfulness toward us is great. (See Lamentations 3:22–23.)

According to Isaiah 53, God deliberately and purposefully allowed His only Son to endure the "fine beating" of the Perfumer's mortar and pestle. Jesus was "*stricken…smitten…afflicted…pierced through…crushed*" (Isaiah 53:4–5). Why? Because God enjoyed seeing Jesus suffer? No! Because He took delight in His Son's pain? No! Because He knew that through the suffering and pain, Jesus would become a sweet-smelling sacrifice that would save the world.

It's crucial to note that Jesus was not a victim. He chose to undergo the crushing process, because He knew the joy that awaited Him. He could have said no. He could have refused. He could have walked away. But He chose to submit Himself to His Father's will, and because He did, we have the promise of everlasting life with Him.

Like Jesus, we are not victims. We can choose to submit to God's will and allow Him to use the circumstances of our life—even the hardships we encounter—to transform us into a fine fragrance. Or, we can refuse and choose to become fearful, angry, resentful, and bitter. He wants our worship to come forth freely, not in spite of but because of the piercing, sorrow, and crushing we undergo. He is preparing us to be the incense that, when placed upon the gold altar of our lives, will arise before Him as a sweet-smelling aroma and be consumed in His presence.

As the priests of our temple, it's up to us to offer our lives as incense to Him and place ourselves as this incense on the golden altar of our heart. God won't force us to become as sweet-smelling sacrifices to Him. This isn't the pattern He's provided in Scripture. Take a look, and you will see that God did very little in the tabernacle. The priests offered the sacrifices. The priests tended to the golden lampstand. The priests made the bread. The priests put the incense on the altar.

God doesn't create an atmosphere of worship; we do. So often, we wait for God to show up in our quiet times or in our worship services at church, and we're disappointed when it doesn't seem as though He's made an appearance. We forget that it's up to us to create an atmosphere of worship for God.

This is the pilgrimage I've been on ever since that morning in the hotel when I cried out to Him, "Lord, I want to know You. I don't want just to know *about* You; I want to *know* You!"

When we examine the combination of these ingredients and compare them to the pattern God has established for our prayer life, we hear Him saying that He wants our worship to come freely. He's not looking for a parade leader in the church who tells us when to stand up, speak up, raise our hands, sit down, sing praise, or pray. Instead, He wants our worship to simply flow from the depths of our heart—from our brokenness; from our piercings and sorrows—on a daily basis.

I believe God wants us to prepare ourselves in the same way that the priests prepared the incense—not to be crushed but to be a fragrant offering before the Lord. Then, when we put our incense on the altar, it will rise up before Him as a sweet-smelling aroma and be consumed by the coals from the fire on the altar of our heart.

Incense was a type of the glory that filled the house of God. Again, incense is something we offer on the altar; God doesn't do it. Remember, He did very little in the tabernacle or temple. Look at the pattern. Look at the picture. The priests offered the sacrifices. The priests washed the sacrifices and themselves. The priests tended to the golden lampstand. The priests made and changed the bread on the table of showbread. The priests put the incense on the altar. God simply allowed His presence to fill the place so that His glory could be revealed.

The atmosphere we create through our prayers and worship is created by us, but it is created for God.

Golden Bowls of Incense

Jesus told us to store up for ourselves treasure in heaven. (See Matthew 6:20.) I believe that all of the Israelites' worship, all of the priests' prayers and intercession, all of the incense from the gold altar, and all of the worship, prayers, intercession, and incense that we have offered to God have been preserved in heaven for eternity.

> *When He had taken the book, the four living creatures and the twenty-four elders fell down before the Lamb, each one holding a harp and golden bowls full of incense, which are the prayers of the saints....Another angel came and stood at the altar, holding a golden censer; and much incense was given to him, so that he might add it to the prayers of all the saints on the golden altar which was before the throne. And the smoke of the incense, with the prayers of the saints, went up before God out of the angel's hand.* (Revelation 5:8; 8:3–4)

As we endure crushing, hardship, and pain in this life, may we continue to make sacrifices of praise to God, remembering that...

For this reason I also suffer these things, but I am not ashamed; for I know whom I have believed and I am convinced that He is able to guard what I have entrusted to Him until that day. (2 Timothy 1:12)

Amen.

Beyond the Veil

Well, my friend, we have journeyed far together on this pathway into God's presence. We have come through the gates and into the outer court with the bronze altar and the bronze laver. We have climbed the stairs with our Psalms of Ascent and moved into the inner court with the gold lampstand, the table of showbread, and the altar of incense.

And now the veil, and what lies beyond, awaits us.

As we prepare to journey even further into intimacy with God, know that the only reason we are able to enter into the Holy of Holies is because Jesus Christ, our High Priest, leads the way.

Digging Deeper

1. Of the five incense ingredients listed in Exodus 30, which one best reflects who you are and your life experiences? Why?

2. Describe a time when you felt as though God were the Perfumer and you were being finely ground with His mortar and pestle. During that season, was it hard for you to believe in God's love, compassion, mercy, and faithfulness? Why or why not?

3. Do you ever feel like a victim because of your circumstances? Read Romans 8:37. How can you apply this truth to your life?

4. Spend time with God, worshipping Him. Tell Him how you feel about being as incense to Him. Confess any fear, anger, resentment, or bitterness you may have toward Him. Ask Him to show you how He wants you to create an atmosphere of worship so that you can be blessed by His presence.

PART IV

THE JOURNEY'S REWARD

18

OUR HIGH PRIEST

"But when Christ appeared as a high priest...He entered the holy place once for all."
—Hebrews 9:11–12

So far, in our journey together on the pathway leading to God's presence, we've explored how we first pass through the "gates" leading to our body, soul, and spirit. We've dug for the buried treasure and hidden mysteries in the "outer court," where we receive the atoning blood of Jesus' sacrifice on the "bronze altar" of our heart. At the "bronze laver," we experienced the lifelong process of being made holy through *the washing of water with the word* (Ephesians 5:26).

Our journey has continued as we've explored God's pictures and patterns with the "stairway of praise" and then moved on into the holy space of the "inner court" of our heart, where the "golden lampstand" shines the light of God's Word; we're nourished by Jesus, our "living Bread"; and we become as "incense" to God, offering up our worship and intercession before Him. We've moved beyond the outer court and through the inner court.

Having come this far, we are separated from the true intimacy of God's presence by only one thing: the veil separating the inner court from the Holy of Holies. In the wilderness tabernacle and in Solomon's temple, the only person permitted to go beyond the veil was the high priest.

How sad it would be, how desperate our longing would be, if we were destined to forever remain in the inner court and were forbidden to enter the Holy of Holies, where God's presence dwells. Thankfully, we have a High Priest who has torn the veil away so that we may abide forever in intimacy with Him!

Before we move beyond the veil into this awesome place of deep and abiding intimacy with the One whose greatest desire is to be known and loved by us, there is still more treasure buried in Scripture—more mysteries I want us to discover together.

Pictures, Patterns, Mysteries, and Types

By now you have a clear understanding of how God uses the natural to reveal the spiritual. He invites us to decipher the mysteries and treasures within the pictures and patterns He has buried in His Word.

Another name for these pictures and patterns is "types." When searching for the "types" found in Scripture, we can study the history of God's people in the Old Testament in order to learn truths that apply to the revelation of Jesus Christ in the New Testament. These are truths God has deliberately and purposefully included in His Word so that we can uncover the deep meaning He wants us to understand and apply to our lives today.

For example, Moses was a "type" of Christ. Just as Moses was the leader of God's chosen people, so is Jesus Christ our Leader and the Head of the church. Just as Moses led the Israelites out of slavery and into a new land, according to God's covenant with their father Abraham, so does Jesus set us free from the bondage of our enemy and bring us into a place full of promise and hope as we live in a covenant relationship with our heavenly Father.

Whereas Moses was the author of the law, Jesus was the Author of the gospel of grace and mercy. Moses was a mediator between the Israelites and God, and Jesus is the Mediator between God and all of mankind. Moses was the first great prophet, and the testimony of Jesus Himself is the *"spirit of prophecy"* (Revelation 19:10).

Through this example, we can clearly see how God established Moses as a "type" of Christ. Now let's look at another type in Scripture that has great significance for us as we prepare to enter the Holy of Holies and encounter God's presence.

The Day of Atonement

When God gave Moses the pattern for building the tabernacle, He also provided specific instructions for Aaron's service as the first high priest over the Israelites. (See Exodus 28–29; 30:22–33; 39; Leviticus 7:28–9:24; 16:1–34.) God outlined detailed directions for what Aaron was to wear, how he was to be consecrated, how he was to perform the sacrifices, and when he was permitted to go into the Holy of Holies.

Just as in Old Testament times, the Day of Atonement is still observed today, prior to the Feast of Tabernacles, during September or October on our Gregorian calendar. This day is considered to be the holiest day of the year, when Jews and believers around the world set aside twenty-four hours to fast, pray, and repent of the sins they have committed against God.

However, when the tabernacle and the temple were still places of worship and sacrifice, the solemn observation of the Day of Atonement also included animal sacrifices, purification, and the anointing of God's mercy seat inside the Holy of Holies with blood from the animals that had been slain.

We learned in chapter 10 that there is power in the blood, because the life is in the blood (see Leviticus 17:11), and without the shedding of blood, there is no forgiveness of sin (see Hebrews 9:22). God's holy standard required that blood be shed in order for the Israelites' sins to be forgiven, and as the high priest, Aaron alone bore the burden of performing the sacrifices, first to atone for his own sins, and then to atone for the sins of the people. (See Leviticus 16:6–17.)

No one was to be in the tabernacle when Aaron entered the Holy of Holies, and even Aaron himself couldn't come into God's holy presence anytime he wanted; only on the Day of Atonement was he permitted to do so. Disregarding this commandment would have resulted in his death.

The LORD said to Moses: "Tell your brother Aaron that he shall not enter at any time into the holy place inside the veil, before the mercy seat which is on the ark, or he will die; for I will appear in the cloud over the mercy seat." (Leviticus 16:2)

According to Leviticus 16, each year on the Day of Atonement, Aaron would…

+ prepare himself for what lay ahead.

+ purify himself according to God's instructions.

+ clothe himself, first in the ornate, colorful garb of the high priest, and then in white, to symbolize humility and purity before God.

+ sacrifice a bull for his own sin and the sins of his household.

+ offer a ram as a burnt offering.

+ select two goats, designating one as the "scapegoat," bearing the sins of the people and released alive into the wilderness; the other was offered as a burnt offering.

+ anoint the horns and sides of the golden altar of incense in the inner court with blood.

+ take coals and incense from the golden altar, enter the Holy of Holies, and place the incense before the mercy seat as an act of intercession.

+ sprinkle the mercy seat with blood from the bull and the goat, in order to purify them from the people's sins.

+ return to the outer court and lay his hands on the head of the scapegoat, confess the sins of the people over it, and then send it into the wilderness, where the goat would wander until its death.

For as long as the Israelites had a tabernacle or a temple in which to worship, these rituals were performed by the high priest on the Day of Atonement, year after year.

Let's dig now for the buried treasure God has hidden in the pattern of the high priest and the animal sacrifices.

The Buried Treasure of the High Priest

Just as Moses was a type of Christ, so were Aaron and the animal sacrifices types of how Jesus would one day sacrifice Himself on the cross on our behalf and also serve as our High Priest. Like Aaron and the animal sacrifices, Jesus…

+ prepared Himself for what lay ahead.

+ kept Himself pure before God.

+ became for us our sin offering.

+ purified the temple in heaven with His blood.

+ was the "Scapegoat" on whose head our sins were laid.

Like Aaron, Jesus was anointed and set apart for His role as high priest. (See Exodus 28:41; Mark 14:3.) Both wore the linen robe of the high priest (see Leviticus 16:4; John 19:23), and both bore the twelve tribes of Israel on their breast—Aaron in the natural, by wearing the priestly ephod as God had commanded (see Exodus 28:4), and Jesus in the spiritual, by bearing our cause before the Father (see John 17).

Whenever the Israelites stopped to set up camp as they traveled through the wilderness, Aaron was to establish his personal camp to the east. By doing so, the Israelites' high priest was always positioned by the single entrance leading into the tabernacle. This is a picture of how Jesus, as our High Priest is *the* entrance, *the* gate, the *only* way by which we can enter into God's presence. (See John 10:7–9 NIV; 14:6.)

Both Aaron and Jesus stood in the gap in intercession on behalf of the people (see Leviticus 16:12–13, 16; Hebrews 7:25), and just as Aaron entered the Holy of Holies to cleanse it from the sins of the people with a blood sacrifice (see Leviticus 16:14–16), so, too, Jesus entered the Holy of Holies in the heavenly tabernacle and purified it with His blood. (See Hebrews 9:11–12, 23–24.)

While there are many meaningful similarities between Aaron as the Israelites' high priest and Jesus as our High Priest, there is a significant difference. The blood of the animal sacrifices offered in the outer court to atone for the sins of the people and applied to the mercy seat in the Holy of Holies protected them from God's wrath. However, although the blood covered the sins of the people, it couldn't permanently wipe away their guilt. (See Hebrews 10:3–4, 11.) Because of this, Aaron and all the priests who followed him had to repeat the same sacrifices and rituals day after day in the outer court and year after year on the Day of Atonement.

However, when Jesus died on the cross as God's sacrificial Lamb to take away the sins of the whole world, He died once for all!

> *Every priest stands daily ministering and offering time after time the same sacrifices, which can never take away sins; but He, having offered one sacrifice for sins for all time,* SAT DOWN AT THE RIGHT HAND OF GOD, *waiting from that time onward* UNTIL HIS ENEMIES BE MADE A FOOTSTOOL FOR HIS FEET. *For by one offering He has perfected for all time those who are sanctified.*
> (Hebrews 10:11–14)

There was no longer a need for the temple sacrifices at the bronze altar or a high priest to go into the Holy of Holies. The highest of all priests had eternally and permanently wiped away the sins of all those who would accept His sacrificial death as the one and only atonement for their sins. His work on the cross was a finished work.

"It Is Finished!"

One of the most profound and moving types for Christ in the Old Testament lies hidden in the blood sacrifice of the outer court.

After the animal had been slain and placed on the altar, the priest would watch and wait until the offering had been consumed in the fire. Then he would stretch out his arms and cry out, "It is finished!"

In the same way, when Jesus was hanging on the cross with His arms outstretched, He cried out, right as He died, *"It is finished!"* (John 19:30). The Pharisees, Sadducees, and maybe even the high priest Caiaphas, who witnessed this powerful moment, surely would have understood the significance of Jesus' final words.

Perhaps there were those at Jesus' crucifixion who also were at the Jordan River when the crowds had come to John to be baptized. With His last breath, Jesus clearly identified Himself with the sin offerings sacrificed on the bronze altar, fulfilling John's prophetic words when he pointed to Jesus and declared, *"Behold, the Lamb of God who takes away the sin of the world!"* (John 1:29).

At the precise moment that Jesus hung His head and died, an amazing miracle occurred in the temple, to which both Matthew and Mark testify: *"The veil of the temple was torn in two from top to bottom"* (Matthew 27:51; Mark 15:38).

Why was this torn veil a miracle, and what significance does it have for us today? Let's dig a little deeper to discover some more buried treasure.

The Veil Is Torn

There were two veils used in Moses' wilderness tabernacle—the outer veil, or the first veil, which served as the doorway leading from the outer court into the inner court; and the inner veil, or the second veil, which separated the inner court from the Holy of Holies. This is the veil that was torn when Jesus died, and we find a description of it in Exodus 26:31–33:

> You shall make a veil of blue and purple and scarlet material and fine twisted linen; it shall be made with cherubim, the work of a skillful workman. You shall hang it on four pillars of acacia overlaid with gold, their hooks also being of gold, on four sockets of silver. You shall hang up the veil under the clasps, and shall bring in the ark of the testimony there within the veil; and the veil shall serve for you as a partition between the holy place and the holy of holies.

By the time the tabernacle had been replaced with the temple in Jerusalem as the center of Jewish worship, the construction of the veil had evolved into an amazing process described in the *Mishnah*, the written tradition of Jewish rabbinical law.

I had always pictured the temple veil as having been made from a flimsy, lacy, or gauzy kind of material, but boy, was I wrong! According to rabbinical teaching, the veil was 60 feet high, 30 feet wide, and "a hands-breadth thick" (between 4 and 6 inches)! In order to determine if a veil was of a high enough quality for use in the temple, it would be hooked up to two teams of oxen pulling in opposite directions in an attempt to tear it apart. Only those veils which withstood this extreme test were used.

The temple veil had survived this endurance test, yet it still was torn from top to bottom at the moment of Jesus' death. Unbelievable! In addition, the veil was torn from top to bottom; even if, by some form of superhuman strength, the priests had somehow managed to tear it in two, it would have been impossible for them to have reached up sixty feet to tear it from the top. Only God could perform such a miracle! What does this mean, and why did God do this?

The author of Hebrews gives us our answer:

> Therefore, brethren, since we have confidence to enter the holy place by the blood of Jesus, by a new and living way which He inaugurated for us through

the veil, that is, His flesh, and since we have a great priest over the house of God, Let us draw near with a sincere heart in full assurance of faith, having our hearts sprinkled clean from an evil conscience and our bodies washed with pure water. (Hebrews 10:19–22)

Just as Jesus' flesh was torn to make a pathway for us into God's presence, so did God supernaturally tear the veil that separated us from the Holy of Holies, so that we could draw near to Him in faith.

Now I want us to pause for a moment and read a very unusual passage in the New Testament.

Behind the second veil there was a tabernacle which is called the Holy of Holies, having a golden altar of incense, and the Ark of the Covenant covered on all sides with gold, in which was a golden jar holding the manna, and Aaron's rod which budded, and the tables of the covenant; and above it were the cherubim of glory overshadowing the mercy seat; but of these things we cannot now speak in detail. (Hebrews 9:3–5)

When I read these verses, I said to myself, *Wait a minute! That's not right! The altar of incense was in the inner court. How in the world did it get moved into the Holy of Holies?*

Well, I don't know the answer to this question for sure, but I do know that "God is not a man, that He should lie" (Numbers 23:19). So, if the Word says that the golden altar of incense from the temple was now in the Holy of Holies, then it must be true.

I believe that when Jesus said, *"It is finished!"* (John 19:30) and the veil separating the inner court from the Holy of Holies was torn in two, God supernaturally moved the altar of incense into the Holy of Holies. By doing so, He would have revealed yet another pattern to us: It's our worship, offered freely from the depths of our heart and out of our brokenness and crushing, that brings us into God's presence.

By His death on the cross, our High Priest, Jesus Christ, paid the highest price to allow us access to the very Holy of Holies. God Himself tore the veil to demonstrate that His blood requirement for the remission of our sins had been forever satisfied through His Son's sacrificial death.

No longer must we be separated from an intimate relationship with Him. Instead of being terrified of God striking us dead for entering the Holy of Holies in an unworthy manner, we can have confidence based on the atoning work of Jesus Christ that our heavenly Father lovingly invites us to freely and boldly enter into His presence.

Will you accept His invitation?

Digging Deeper

1. Based on what you now understand about "types" in Scripture, make a list of the ways that the animal sacrifices were a type, or a pattern, of Jesus as our sacrifice.

2. Hebrews 10:14 says, *"For by one offering He has perfected for all time those who are sanctified."* This means that if Jesus Christ is your Lord, then you have been *"perfected for all time."* Does the way in which you view yourself reflect this truth? How so?

3. Reread Hebrews 10:19–22, in which God invites you to boldly enter into the intimacy of His presence. Describe how you feel when you think about entering into the "Holy of Holies." Are you bold? Fearful? Unsure? Thrilled? Intimidated? Eager? Ashamed?

4. Spend time telling the Lord how you feel about coming into His presence and being in an intimate relationship with Him. Ask Him to help you feel His deep love for you as He draws you closer to Himself.

19

BEYOND THE VEIL

"Therefore, brethren, since we have confidence to enter the holy place by the blood of Jesus, by a new and living way...let us draw near with a sincere heart in full assurance of faith."
—Hebrews 10:19–20, 22

The pathway on which we've been journeying together has led us beyond the veil and into the holiest of all places—the very presence of God. Our desire to know Him and be known by Him has brought us to this moment.

As I shared with you in chapter 1, my own journey began years ago, when I was desperately hungry to experience a deeper intimacy in my relationship with the Lord. I wasn't content where I was in my walk with Him. I knew there was more, and I was determined to pursue Him with passionate abandon.

That morning in the hotel coffee shop, the Lord spoke these five words to my spirit:

Repent. Praise. Worship. Offering. Sacrifice.

Together, you and I have searched out some of the vital pictures, patterns, and mysteries God has hidden in His Word. We've discovered how the outer court of the tabernacle was a place of *repentance*. We've unearthed the treasure of *praise* in the stairs leading to the temple, and we've mined the "gold" of *worship* in the inner court as God chose to reveal them through the golden lampstand, the table of showbread, and the golden altar of incense.

Now it is time for us to explore the mystery of the Holy of Holies, which is the ultimate place of *offering* and *sacrifice*.

A Place of Offering

The Holy of Holies in the wilderness tabernacle was a room with dimensions that formed a perfect cube: 10 cubits long by 10 cubits wide by 10 cubits high (15 feet × 15 feet × 15 feet.) It's interesting to consider this "cube" where the presence of God dwelt on earth, and to contrast it with the description of heaven in Revelation 21:16:

> *The city is laid out as a square, and its length is as great as the width; and he measured the city with the rod, fifteen hundred miles; its length and width and height are equal.*

John, the author of Revelation, describes the city of God as being laid out as a cube in three dimensions, meaning its length and width are equal to its height.

During the forty years that the Israelites spent in the wilderness, the presence of God hovered over the Holy of Holies in the form of a pillar of fire by night and a cloud by day. (See Numbers 9:15–23.)

This holiest of all rooms contained only one piece of furniture at the time: the ark of the covenant. When God gave Moses the instructions regarding its construction, He said He would *meet* with His people and *speak* to them before the ark of the covenant and tell them what to do.

> *There I will **meet** with you; and from above the mercy seat, from between the two cherubim which are upon the ark of the testimony, I will **speak** to you about all that I will give you in **commandment** for the sons of Israel.*
>
> (Exodus 25:22)

Exodus 25:10–22 describes the ark in great detail. (See Reference figure C-1.) It was…

- a box measuring 3 feet 9 inches long, 2 feet, 3 inches wide, and 2 feet, 3 inches high.
- made of acacia wood.
- overlaid with pure gold inside and out, with a gold molding all the way around.
- fitted with gold rings on the four corners to hold the acacia wood poles (also overlaid with gold) used for transporting it.

The lid of the ark was 3 feet 9 inches long by 2 feet 3 inches wide. Called the "mercy seat," the entire lid was made of pure gold and served as the throne for God's presence. On either end were two cherubim (worshipping angels) made of hammered gold, which sat facing each other with their outstretched wings covering the mercy seat.

According to God's commandments, the ark contained three items that were to serve as constant reminders of the Israelites' frailty and dependence on God, and His abiding faithfulness to His covenant people:

- A jar of manna (see Exodus 16:33)
- The tablets of the Ten Commandments (see Exodus 25:16; 34:29)
- Aaron's rod that had budded (see Numbers 17:1–10)

As I shared with you in the previous chapter, once a year, on the Day of Atonement, the high priest would enter the Holy of Holies to offer up incense to God and to sprinkle the blood from the sacrifices on the mercy seat, thereby purifying it from the people's sins.

The desire of God's heart has always been to draw His children into increasingly deeper levels of intimacy with Him. He provided Moses with a detailed description of the Holy of Holies for two reasons: (1) to convey His demands for holiness, and (2) to reveal the pattern for experiencing the rich rewards of intimacy with Him.

Let's dig now for the treasure God has buried in this most holy place.

We Are the Offering

Because God provided Moses with clear directions for the Holy of Holies and the ark of the covenant, it's clear that He wants to meet with us, speak to us, and give us commandments (show us what to do) in this place of stillness and intimacy.

> *There will I **meet** with you; and from above the mercy seat, from between the two cherubim which are upon the ark of the testimony, I will **speak** to you about all that I will give you in **commandment** for the sons of Israel.*
>
> (Exodus 25:22)

Throughout Scripture, God invites us to draw near to Him and be with Him:

> *The LORD is near to all who call upon Him, to all who call upon Him in truth.* (Psalm 145:18)

> *I have loved you with an everlasting love; therefore I have drawn you with lovingkindness.* (Jeremiah 31:3)

> *Draw near to God and He will draw near to you.* (James 4:8)

But, through the millennia, God's standard for holiness has never changed; even as He invites us to know Him intimately, He still requires "blood" and "incense" for us to enter His presence and be with Him.

Just as the high priest brought the coals and incense from the golden altar into the Holy of Holies (see Reference figure C-2), so must each one of us serve as the priest of our own "temple," entering into God's holy presence bearing the sweet-smelling incense of our worship. And just as the high priest anointed the mercy seat with the blood of the animal sacrifice to cleanse it from the sins of the people, so must we enter the Holy of Holies anointed with the cleansing blood of the Lord Jesus Christ.

Unless we maintain a posture of worship and humility before Him, entering His presence is impossible. Without the sacrificial blood of Jesus covering us, we *cannot* come into the Holy of Holies, because His holiness is too magnificent; our sinfulness is too great.

When we enter into the holiness of God's presence, we're entering a place of *offering*. In the outer court, one way we draw near to God is by bringing Him our tithes and offerings, while we also receive the offering Jesus made on our behalf. However, within the Holy of Holies, *we become the offering* as we humbly submit our lives to our loving God and enter into in an intimate relationship with Him.

True Intimacy

In many ways, intimacy with the Lord is like the intimate relationship between a husband and wife. When a married couple has a relationship that's built on a solid foundation of love, trust, and mutual respect, the closeness of their relationship is reflected in the most intimate moments of their marriage. In the Bible, the word used to describe this is the Hebrew word *yada'*, meaning "to know, perceive, recognize, to know intimately."

Yada' is used when Scripture says that Adam *"knew Eve his wife"* (Genesis 4:1 NKJV) and that Elkanah *"knew Hannah his wife"* (1 Samuel 1:19 NKJV).

This is the kind of love relationship God desires to have with each one of us—a relationship characterized by true knowledge and intimacy—and when He says, *"Before I formed you in the womb I knew you, and before you were born I consecrated you"* (Jeremiah 1:5), it's this same word, yada', He uses.

God revealed a pattern for intimacy with Him through the words of the apostle Paul, as he described the mystery of the marriage relationship:

> So husbands ought also to love their own wives as their own bodies. He who loves his own wife loves himself; for no one ever hated his own flesh, but nourishes and cherishes it, just as Christ also does the church, because we are members of His body. FOR THIS CAUSE A MAN SHALL LEAVE HIS FATHER AND MOTHER, AND SHALL CLEAVE TO HIS WIFE; AND THE TWO SHALL BECOME ONE FLESH. **This mystery is great; but I am speaking with reference to Christ and the church.**
> (Ephesians 5:28–32)

When a husband and wife truly "know" one another, they aren't just aware of their spouse's favorite color, the restaurant where he or she likes to eat, or even the secrets they share with no one but one another. For a man and a woman to be truly intimate, they must know and experience intimacy with one another on *every* level of their relationship—emotionally, mentally, and physically.

The sad thing is that so many people have a false sense of intimacy in their marriage. As husbands and wives, it's easy to think that because we watch TV together, talk about the kids, make vacation plans, or enjoy the marriage bed occasionally, we have an intimate marital relationship. But this simply isn't so. There is a difference between companionship and intimacy. For there to be *true* intimacy in marriage, a husband and wife must...

+ honor their covenant to one another by "leaving and cleaving."

+ be eternally faithful to each other.

+ devote special attention to one another.

+ spend meaningful time together.

+ prefer one another's needs over and above their own needs.

+ share the thoughts and feelings of their innermost being.

+ offer themselves to one another in times of intimate, selfless abandon.

+ experience the joy of being fully known as they lovingly "lose themselves" in one another.

It's the same way in our relationship with God: Many of us also have a false sense of intimacy with Him. It's easy to believe that because we go to church, talk to God, read His Word, serve Him faithfully, and even experience great times of praise and worship, we know Him intimately. But much more is required than these practices if we are to have an intimate relationship with God. There's a difference between *knowing about* God and *knowing* God.

In chapter 4, I shared how God wants us to bring Him our *all*. However, our *all* isn't just our time, treasure, and talents. In the Holy of Holies, we offer *ourselves* to the Lord without distraction. We offer our very being to Him with abandon. In the Holy of Holies, we lose ourselves in the magnitude of His deep, abiding love for us. In the stillness of this place, we are fully known, and we experience true intimacy with the Lord.

But the offering of ourselves to God requires *sacrifice*.

A Place of Sacrifice

In the outer court, *Jesus* was the sacrifice, having suffered both horrifying physical torture and, even worse, the unimaginable pain of having His heavenly Father turn away from Him while He was on the cross.

But in the Holy of Holies, *we* are the sacrifice. We offer ourselves by sacrificing the only thing we really have to give Him: our very lives. As we come into His presence to be alone with Him in intimate times of worship, we *"die daily"* (1 Corinthians 15:31).

Hundreds of priests served God by fulfilling their duties in the outer court of the temple, but only one priest was permitted to enter the Holy of Holies. In the outer and inner courts, the high priest ministered on behalf of the people, but in the Holy of Holies, he ministered to God.

In the same way, in the outer court—and even in the inner court—of our spiritual journey with the Lord, we use our time, talents, and treasure to serve the Lord by ministering to His people and winning lost souls for Christ's kingdom. However, when I go into the Holy of Holies, I go in *alone*. In the very presence of the Lord, there is no room for anyone or anything except Him and me.

We too easily confuse ministry activity with intimacy. We can be so busy doing things *for* God that we're too busy to spend time *with* God. I believe that, sadly, most of us spend our lives serving the Lord as "outer-court priests." But this isn't what He desires for us. God loves us so much that He wants to be alone with us in a place of intimacy. He calls each of us to join Him in the hidden place of the Holy of Holies, where no one sees us and no one can flatter us for all our hard work.

> *But you, when you pray, go into your inner room, close your door and pray to your Father who is in secret, and your Father who sees what is done in secret will reward you.* (Matthew 6:6)

As we sacrifice our busyness and the empty words of others' opinions in order to enter into the secret place of the Holy of Holies, our heavenly Father will be glorified, and we will be blessed with the rich reward of an intimate relationship with Him.

No Sweat!

In Ezekiel's vision of the temple, God reveals through the priests and the details of their clothing yet another pattern of what He requires of those who desire intimacy with Him:

> *They shall come near to My table to minister to Me and keep My charge. It shall be that when they enter at the gates of the inner court, they shall be clothed with linen garments; and wool shall not be on them while they are ministering in the gates of the inner court and in the house. Linen turbans shall be on their heads and linen undergarments shall be on their loins;* **they shall not gird themselves with anything which makes them sweat.**
> (Ezekiel 44:16–18)

God said that the priests would come near to *"minister"* to Him. The word used for *"minister"* is the Hebrew word *sharath*, which means "to attend as a servant or worshipper; to serve or wait on." Like the temple priests, we are to serve God in quiet times of waiting on Him in worship.

Why did God command the priests who went into the Holy of Holies to wear linen rather than wool? Because He didn't want them to sweat! Sweat represents our flesh and the act of striving in our own strength to "make things happen." God never anoints the work of our flesh; there is no place for it in the Holy of Holies. God is Spirit, and we must worship Him in spirit and in truth (see John 4:24), not in flesh and the self-deception of our own strength. Those works that we produce as a result of our own "sweat" will amount to nothing but wood, hay, and straw.

> *For no man can lay a foundation other than the one which is laid, which is Jesus Christ. Now if any man builds on the foundation with gold, silver, precious stones, wood, hay, straw, each man's work will become evident; for the day will show it because it is to be revealed with fire, and the fire itself will test the quality of each man's work. If any man's work which he has built on it remains, he will receive a reward.* (1 Corinthians 3:11–14)

As believers, we're too well-acquainted with trying to produce great things for God by the sweat of our brow. For this reason, refusing to strive is one of the greatest sacrifices we can make as we move into increasingly deeper levels of relationship with the Lord.

Deep within our spirit resides the Holy of Holies, the place where God waits for us to offer ourselves to Him in worship. All the things we do for Him in ministry are worthless compared to the sacrifice of humility and brokenness before Him.

> *For You do not delight in sacrifice, otherwise I would give it; You are not pleased with burnt offering. The sacrifices of God are a broken spirit; a broken and a contrite heart, O God, You will not despise.*   (Psalm 51:16–17)

While our times of intimate worship with the Lord may include Scripture, singing, and prayer, sometimes He simply wants us to offer to Him the sacrifice of our busyness, works, and sweat, so that we may just be with Him in quietness, stillness, and silence.

> *In repentance and rest you will be saved, in quietness and trust is your strength.*   (Isaiah 30:15)

> *The LORD is good to those who wait for Him, to the person who seeks Him. It is good that he waits silently for the salvation of the LORD.*
>   (Lamentations 3:25–26)

The Power of Transformation

So often, what motivates us to have a relationship with God is our need. We may go through the motions of worship, but if we're honest, the real cry of our heart is, "Give me this, God," or "I need that, Lord." This isn't relationship, and it's certainly not intimacy. The truth is that although God loves us and is heartbroken over our desperate neediness, He doesn't respond to our need; He responds to our faith-filled, loving obedience and the intimacy of our relationship with Him.

When my grandkids call me at the office, I don't care what I'm doing, what meeting I'm in, or who I'm talking to; my assistant knows to put that call through to me right away. Why? Because of the intimate relationship I have with my grandchildren.

The same is true of our relationship with God. He isn't some far-off, distant God who wants to hide Himself from His children. No, God is a God who is near to us: *"Am I a God who is near,' declares the LORD, 'and not a God afar off?'"* (Jeremiah 23:23).

My heart is crying out for *more* of God, *more* of His presence, *more* intimacy, *more* relationship, and *more* power. But power comes through transformation alone, and transformation comes only through intimacy with Him. Intimacy is birthed from relationship, and relationship is the result of spending time in His presence.

The only way we will have a powerful spiritual life is by spending time in God's presence. Transformation is a process; a pattern; one building block resting upon another.

When we…

+ offer ourselves to God with abandon,

+ die daily to self,

+ sacrifice our striving and simply come to Him in brokenness, and

+ seek to be alone with Him in intimate times of worship,

…then He responds to the cries of our heart: *"Call to Me and I will answer you, and I will tell you great and mighty things, which you do not know"* (Jeremiah 33:3).

As we wait on the Lord and give ourselves as an *offering* and a *sacrifice* to Him in times of worship, He responds to the cries of our heart and blesses us:

Therefore the LORD longs to be gracious to you, and therefore He waits on high to have compassion on you. For the LORD is a God of justice; how blessed are all those who long for Him. O people in Zion, inhabitant in Jerusalem, you will weep no longer. He will surely be gracious to you at the sound of your cry; when He hears it, He will answer you. (Isaiah 30:18–19)

The desire of God's heart is to *meet* with us and *speak* to us in the intimacy of the Holy of Holies. Will you choose to meet Him there?

Digging Deeper

1. According to Exodus 25:22, God wants you to draw near to Him in worship so that He can meet with you and speak to you. Are you eager to do this? Why or why not?

2. Paul uses the analogy of the marriage relationship to describe the intimate relationship the Lord wants to have with you. Are you comfortable with this comparison? Why or why not?

3. God makes it clear that there is to be no "sweating" in His presence. Which of the following statements do you most identify with? What does that say about your relationship with the Lord?

4. "I am working very hard for the Lord and His kingdom, and so I tend to be busy, overworked, stressed, and tired."

5. "I am spending lots of time worshipping the Lord, ministering to Him, and just being with Him in quietness, stillness, and silence."

6. Spend time with the Lord. Read Hebrews 10:18–22. Trust that because of Jesus' blood, you can enter into the Holy of Holies and draw near to God in faith. Receive His amazing love and His 100 percent acceptance of you as His child. Tell Him how much you love Him and desire to go deeper in an intimate relationship with Him. Worship Him in stillness. Wait on Him. Listen for what He wants to say to you in the silence.

20

THIRTY, SIXTY, OR ONE HUNDREDFOLD?

"And others fell on good soil and yielded a crop, some a hundredfold, some sixty, and some thirty. He who has ears, let him hear."
—Matthew 13:8–9

Y ou and I were created to worship God.

The mystery He has revealed through the wilderness tabernacle and Solomon's temple—the outer court with the bronze altar and the bronze laver; the inner court with the golden lampstand, table of showbread, and golden altar of incense; the Holy of Holies; and the ark of the covenant—is the pathway leading to His glorious presence.

Only in God's presence do we...

+ experience His tender love.

+ find hope and healing.

+ know the peace that surpasses all understanding.

+ discover true freedom.

+ receive the rich rewards that come only from an intimate relationship with Him.

But if this is true—and I assure you, it is—why do so few of us complete the journey? Why do we resist exploring the pictures, patterns, and mysteries of His Word to find the gold He has buried there for us to discover? Why aren't we pursuing God with all of our heart, soul, mind, and strength?

I believe that while many of us truly desire a more intimate relationship with God, we're unwilling to pay the price to enter the Holy of Holies. Most of us like the *idea* of being intimate with the Lord, but when it comes right down to it, we can't—or won't—respond to the five words God spoke to my spirit:

Repent. Praise. Worship. Offering. Sacrifice.

God's desire is to welcome you into His presence and surround you with His love and mercy. He longs for you to receive all the blessings that come as a result of intimacy with Him. My friend, this is why He has led me to write this book— to help you pursue the pathway to His presence, so that you may know the joy of intimacy with Him.

Barriers to Intimacy

In order to help you move deeper into an intimate relationship with Him, let's look at some of the barriers that could be preventing you from moving from the outer court, through the inner court, and into the Holy of Holies.

1. Fear

Fear of God: many of us are *afraid* to enter into God's presence. Whether due to our upbringing or to erroneous teachings in the church, many people view God as a disapproving father or an angry judge. Although they may be comfortable with the idea of Jesus as their loving Savior and may relate well to Him, they avoid spending time alone with their heavenly Father out of fear of displeasing Him.

Fear of Intimacy: others may be afraid of intimacy. Experience has taught them that intimate relationships are painful and not worth the hurt that is sure to follow if they pursue the pathway to God's presence.

2. Guilt

Some of us won't dare to enter God's presence because we're living in willful disobedience to His Word. Like Adam and Eve, we run away and hide from God because of our sinfulness rather than running to Him for forgiveness and restoration. The sin of deliberate rebellion blocks us from experiencing intimacy with Him.

3. Shame

Some of us are so crippled with shame that we see ourselves as unworthy to be in God's presence. We're ashamed, not necessarily because of any sin we've committed, but because of the sense of unworthiness that engulfs our very nature. Our very identity is one of shame, and because of this, we simply can't believe that God would even want to have an intimate relationship with us.

4. Doubt and Hopelessness

Because of the seeds of doubt the enemy has sown in our minds, some of us question whether God's Word is true, whether His love for us is real, whether He is really good, and whether He will fulfill His promises to us. Our skepticism holds us back from pursuing Him passionately. Doubt inevitably leads to hopelessness, and hopelessness suffocates and deadens our desire for intimacy.

5. Apathy

Some of us are apathetic. Maybe we've tried the "intimacy thing" with God before and found it just didn't work for us. Perhaps we've worked hard to enter His presence, and we're tired of trying. Over time, we've given up pursuing Him, and now we just don't care anymore.

6. Offense

Many believers in the body of Christ have been wounded by family members, friends, coworkers, bosses, church members, ministry leaders, and others. If they fail to truly forgive those who have deeply hurt them, their unforgiveness will turn into bitterness. And as God warns in Scripture, when we refuse to forgive others, we're unable to receive His forgiveness. (See Matthew 6:15; Mark 11:26.) Without forgiveness, we can't experience times of intimacy in His presence.

7. Unfaithfulness

Just as infidelity on the part of one spouse breaks the marriage covenant and strains the relationship, unfaithfulness to the Lord has a negative impact on our relationship with Him. We "cheat on" God when we love the things of this world more than Him and pursue the lusts of our flesh more passionately than the pathway leading to His presence.

8. Selfishness

There as those of us who aren't pursuing intimacy with God simply because we don't *want* to. We refuse to give up our worldly pleasures because the enemy has deceived us into believing that the "boring" things God wants to give us can't compare to the "exciting" things the world has to offer. Rather than Jesus being our Lord, *we* are seated on the throne of our life, and we have no intentions of moving off of it.

9. Insensitivity

Pursuing the things of this world and following after other lovers (see Hosea 2:5–6) instead of pursuing God and intimacy with Him eventually results in our hearts becoming darkened and calloused to Him and His ways. Our spirits become insensitive to His voice and the moving of His Holy Spirit, rendering intimacy with Him impossible.

10. Busyness

An overwhelming number of us are just too busy to pursue an intimate relationship with God. As with a husband and a wife, intimacy takes *time*, but time feels like such a rare commodity. Sure, it would great to hang out in the Holy of Holies, but when we're sitting before the Lord in silence and worshipping Him, other "important" things just aren't getting done.

All of these barriers prevent us from ministering before the Lord in the Holy of Holies. We can't serve Him from a distance, and we can't receive the fullness of His love if we choose to hang out for the rest of our lives in the outer court or even the inner court.

God invites each of us to enter in and experience the rich rewards of intimacy with Him. However, He's not going to force us into an intimate relationship with

Him. He won't hunt us down in the outer court, and He will never drag us kicking and screaming from the inner court into the fullness of His presence.

What He *does* do is extend the invitation and then patiently and lovingly wait for us to accept it. The choice is ours.

"Thirty, Sixty, and a Hundredfold"

If you've been a believer for any length of time, you probably know the parable of the seed sower:

> *Listen to this! Behold, the sower went out to sow; as he was sowing, some seed fell beside the road, and the birds came and ate it up. Other seed fell on the rocky ground where it did not have much soil; and immediately it sprang up because it had no depth of soil. And after the sun had risen, it was scorched; and because it had no root, it withered away. Other seed fell among the thorns, and the thorns came up and choked it, and it yielded no crop. Other seeds fell into the good soil, and as they grew up and increased, they yielded a crop and produced thirty, sixty, and a hundredfold.* (Mark 4:3–9)

Notice that all the seed that fell onto good soil yielded a crop, but not all of the crops were of the same value: some produced thirty times the amount of seeds planted, others resulted in sixty times the amount of seeds sown, while other seeds reaped a *one hundredfold* harvest!

That's a thirty-, sixty-, or one hundredfold return on the seed sower's investment. I don't know about you, but I would much rather receive one hundred times what I sowed than thirty!

In addition to the many hidden treasures in this parable, which is commonly used to illustrate such things as evangelism, the necessity of sowing financial seeds into good ground, and how to thwart the enemy's plan, I believe there is yet another pattern God wants us to discover.

Body, Soul, and Spirit

Genesis 2:7 says, "Then the LORD God formed man of dust from the ground, and breathed into his nostrils the breath of life; and man became a living being."

There are three important things to note in this short verse:

1. God formed man from the dust of the ground.
2. God breathed the breath of life into man.
3. Man became a living being.

God's Spirit gave man his body, his soul, and his spirit.

Then, in 1 Thessalonians 5:23, we read, *"Now may the God of peace Himself sanctify you entirely; and may your spirit and soul and body be preserved complete, without blame at the coming of our Lord Jesus Christ."* Note that Paul named three aspects that compose who we are: our body, our soul, and our spirit.

Our *body* is our physical self that houses our soul and spirit. It's our "earth suit" (someday, we'll live in new, resurrected bodies in heaven!), and it represents the outer court, which is a picture of a *thirtyfold* relationship with the Lord. In the outer court, we accept Jesus as our Savior and are baptized by the water and the Word. This is an essential beginning, but we can't stop there.

Our *soul* is made up of our mind, will, and emotions. It's the part of us that says, "I think," "I will," and "I feel." Our soul influences our body and represents the inner court, which is a picture of a *sixtyfold* relationship with the Lord. In the inner court, we're illuminated by God's Word, and our understanding of Jesus as the Light of the world deepens. We feast on Him—the Bread of Life—and we enjoy of fresh manna as we read the Word daily and as we partake in Communion.

In the inner court, our spiritual life deepens as we communicate with God through the illumination of His Word, and as we pray, worship Him, and allow Him to crush us into a sweet incense that arises before Him. Although our understanding of God and our experience with Him in the inner court is awesome, it is not the full expression of an intimate relationship with Him. There is more!

Our *spirit* is the part of us that is made in God's image. When we accept Jesus Christ as our Lord and Savior, it's our spirit that's instantly justified by His blood, and it's on our spirit that God places the seal of His Holy Spirit. (See Ephesians 1:13.) Our spirit influences our soul, and it represents the Holy of Holies, which is a picture of the *one hundredfold* relationship and experience with the Lord. In this holy place, we're rewarded with His presence, peace, and power. We sense His overwhelming love for us, and our spirit becomes one with His.

I also want to point out to you that in the outer court of the tabernacle, the sun and the moon provided natural light. In the inner court, the light source was candlelight, which was man-made. And in the Holy of Holies, the light source was supernatural, because it was the *shekinah* glory of God Himself that shone in the darkness. From this, we see yet another pattern of the progression of our intimate relationship with God.

One Spirit

When Adam and Eve sinned in the garden, their *spirits* were cut off from God, and they became *"dead in…trespasses and sins"* (Ephesians 2:1). The consequence of their sin is that our body will decay and eventually die forever. However, our soul—our mind, will, and emotions, along with the choices we make—will determine where our spirit (housed in a new body) will spend eternity.

Our intimacy with God is restored only through the sacrifice of His Son on the cross. Just as the bronze altar was the first piece of furniture encountered by the priests in the outer court, so too is Jesus the first step we must take on the pathway to God's presence. Like the animal sacrifices in the outer court, it is only through Jesus' shed blood that we receive forgiveness for our sins.

It's vital to understand that only our spirit—neither our soul nor our body— is capable of direct fellowship with God. As I shared with you in the previous chapter, God is a *Spirit*, and those who desire intimacy with Him must worship Him in *spirit* and in truth. (See John 4:24.) When we accept Jesus' sacrifice made on our behalf as the payment for our sins, it's our spirit that's saved, renewed, and restored to fellowship with God.

Paul wrote to the Corinthians, *"Don't you know that the one who joins himself to a prostitute is one body with her? For He says, 'THE TWO SHALL BECOME ONE FLESH.' But the one who joins himself to the Lord is one spirit with Him"* (1 Corinthians 6:16–17). On the one hand, Paul was warning believers against immorality when he told them to be careful not to be sexually impure. On the other hand, Paul also was making it clear that when we join our spirit with God's spirit, we become one with Him.

When we worship, God intends for all three parts of us to be engaged: body, soul, and spirit. But it's our *spirit* that is one with His, and an intimate relationship is the result. Our body and soul simply aren't capable of this kind of intimacy with the Lord. Only our spirit can have union with God, and this union comes through worship!

More of Him

Some days, I feel as though I take a step forward on the pathway leading to a deepening intimacy with God, and then there are those days when I seem to take a giant step backward. Regardless, I am determined not to live in a thirtyfold relationship with Him.

I don't want to settle for an outer-court experience with Him. Yes, I'm grateful I've been saved by the blood of the Lamb at the bronze altar; yes, I'm glad I've been baptized and washed by the water and the Word at the bronze laver. But this isn't enough for me, and I hope it's not enough for you, either.

To be completely honest, I've spent most of my life living in the inner court and being satisfied with a sixtyfold relationship with the Lord. And the inner court life is wonderful. I've experienced God through the golden lampstand and the illumination of His Word. I've feasted on Jesus as my daily Bread at the table of showbread; I've conformed my will to His; I've offered up my worship and intercession to God at the golden altar, even in the midst of times when I felt like I was being crushed by His mortar and pestle.

But, in recent years, God has graciously led me on the pathway to His presence, and I'm no longer content with a sixtyfold relationship in the inner court. I have experienced firsthand the true intimacy that is found exclusively in the Holy of Holies. I've met with God there. I've offered Him my very life as a living sacrifice.

And as I've ministered to Him in this holy place, He's spoken to me. I've experienced the reality of His presence, peace, and power. I've been enveloped by His love and overwhelmed by His mercy and grace, and I will never again be satisfied with anything less than a one hundredfold relationship.

How about you? Do you want more? More of His presence in your life? More of His peace? More of His power? More intimacy with Him? More?

As you have read this book, has your spirit resounded with a thundering "Yes"? Are you feeling a stirring deep within, a longing for more, a desire to enter into the intimacy of the Holy of Holies, and a hunger to taste for yourself and see that the Lord is good? Or maybe you're wondering if a one hundredfold relationship is even possible. Maybe you want what I'm describing, but you're afraid.

Regardless of where you find yourself on this journey, this is a decision each of us must make for ourselves: *"Multitudes, multitudes in the valley of decision. For the day of the LORD is near in the valley of decision"* (Joel 3:14).

How Far Do You Want to Go?

Know that wherever you are on your journey, God loves you right where you are. He's not impatient with you. He's not frustrated with you. He's not disappointed with you. But He desperately wants you to join Him in the Holy of Holies. He desires you to be in an intimate, one hundredfold relationship with Him. He wants to give you more.

In order to have more of Him, you'll need to decide how far you want to go. Jesus said, *"Blessed are those who hunger and thirst for righteousness, for they shall be satisfied"* (Matthew 5:6). The Greek word used here for *"hunger"* is *peinao*, which means "to be famished; to crave."

Imagine you were starving, and you walked into a restaurant filled with buffet tables covered with food. What would you do? Would you mind your manners and patiently wait your turn in line? Would you carefully use all the right silverware, wipe your mouth with your napkin after each bite, and make sure to chew with your mouth closed? I don't think so. A starving person has no manners. I bet you would run over to those tables and begin feasting ravenously on everything in sight.

In the same way, God wants us to *crave* His presence. However, so many ministry leaders are focused on "politically correct" church behavior. They've taught us to sit quietly with our hands folded, or maybe to raise our hands in the air a little, if an especially powerful praise song is sung.

Sadly, many of us don't even know we're hungry. We're not starving for God's presence because we haven't experienced true intimacy with Him. In fact, we don't really know what this means—we don't know what we're missing. Instead, we're gorging on a steady diet of "junk food" that disguises just how spiritually malnourished we are.

Are you content with being an acquaintance of the Lord's, or are you starving to know Him intimately? Are you just fine with being good friends, or are you famished for His presence? Will you take the next step along the pathway to His presence, or do you prefer to stay right where you are?

If you're willing to abandon yourself to Him as a living sacrifice, and if you're ready—by His grace and with His strength—to overcome the barriers holding you back from an intimate relationship with Him, then it's time for you to press in.

Digging Deeper

1. At the beginning of this chapter, there is a list of barriers to intimacy with the Lord. Review that list and identify one or two of the barriers that are especially challenging for you to overcome. Why are these difficult for you?

2. Consider your current relationship with the Lord. Would you describe yourself as having a thirtyfold, sixtyfold, or one hundredfold relationship with Him? Why? Are you satisfied with where you are, or are you hungry for more?

3. Are you content with being an acquaintance of the Lord's, or are you starving to know Him intimately? Why or why not?

4. Spend time with the Lord right now. Share with Him all of your responses from questions 1 through 3. If you're ready to press in, tell Him so, and ask for His grace and strength to help you overcome every barrier that would keep you from His presence.

21

PRESS IN!

"That I may know Him and the power of His resurrection."
—Philippians 3:10

Well, my friend, we've traveled far together along this pathway leading to God's presence. We began at the gates of Solomon's temple and ended our journey in the Holy of Holies. We've learned much along the way as we explored different pictures and patterns, and we've dug deep for God's hidden treasure buried in the mysteries of His Word.

When Jesus said to the Pharisees, *"If you believed Moses, you would believe Me, for he wrote about Me"* (John 5:46), He spoke correctly. Moses diligently recorded the clear instructions God had given him regarding the construction of the tabernacle, its contents, and their placement within the tabernacle, all the while unaware that he was detailing a prophetic picture of the sacrificial death of the coming Messiah.

I'll invite you to pause for a moment now and form a mental picture of the physical tabernacle. Imagine the contents of the outer court, the inner court, and the Holy of Holies. With your mind's eye, see...

+ the bronze altar in the outer court and the bronze laver behind it.

+ the golden lampstand on the left in the inner court, the table of showbread to the right, and the altar of incense straight ahead.

+ the ark of the covenant in the Holy of Holies.

Do you see how these six pieces of furniture form the shape of a cross? What is the picture God wants us to see in this? The entire tabernacle is a representation of Jesus Christ! He is revealed in each piece of furniture, and when all of these separate pieces are seen in their totality, He is revealed as crucified on our behalf.

But notice that it requires all six pieces of furniture to form the cross. From the bronze altar in the outer court to the ark of the covenant in the Holy of Holies, each one is necessary. If we stop at the bronze laver in the outer court, we don't have the full picture. If we stop at the golden altar of incense in the inner court, we may have a more accurate representation of Jesus, but the picture isn't complete.

What's the pattern?

In order to receive the fullness of Jesus' redeeming work on the cross, we must enter into the Holy of Holies and experience the intimacy of God's presence. It's not enough to be saved. It's not enough to be baptized. It's not enough to be illumined by the Word on a daily basis, take Communion, or even pray and worship. We must abandon ourselves fully to God and offer our lives as a living sacrifice to Him in the Holy of Holies. Anything less denies the fullness of what Jesus died to give us.

So, how do we press into God's presence? How do we deepen the intimacy of our relationship with Him? How do we abide in the Holy of Holies?

The answer to these questions is simple, but it isn't necessarily easy, and it most certainly isn't popular. Like the rich young ruler who went away sad when Jesus told him what would be required of him in order to attain eternal life (see Matthew 19:16–26), many believers shrink back when they learn what is required for them to have an intimate relationship with the Lord.

The tragic truth is that most of the world will not be saved, and most of us who have become believers won't choose to press into an intimate relationship with the Lord. As Jesus said, *"The gate is small and the way is narrow that leads to life, and there are few who find it"* (Matthew 7:14). But you can be one of those few!

Six Principles for Entering Into His Presence

If you're one of the precious few who is choosing to press into God's presence, then I have six principles to share that will help you develop godly habits leading to a more intimate relationship with your heavenly Father.

Principle #1: Have a Dedicated Time

Having a dedicated time each day to spend with the Lord is the first principle for forming the habit of being alone with Him. For me, the best time of day is in the morning. For you, it may be during your lunch break, or maybe it's the last hour of the day. The time of day doesn't really matter. What matters is consistency. Make a daily appointment with Him, and then keep it. Of course, schedules change, and there may be days when your regular quiet time simply isn't possible, but this should be the exception rather than the rule.

Principle #2: Have a Special Place

The second principle for forming the habit of being alone with God is having a special place for your quiet time. Decide where your "Holy of Holies" will be, and then go there every day so that He can *"meet with you…[and] speak with you"* (Exodus 25:22). My special place to be alone with the Lord is in the study of our home. You may prefer a special chair in a corner somewhere, or maybe you have a sunny spot where you like to sit. It doesn't really matter, so long as it's a place that's quiet and peaceful for you.

Principle #3: Be Free from Interruptions

A third principle for developing the habit of entering into God's presence on a daily basis is making sure that your time with Him occurs when and where you can be free from interruptions. We all know what it's like to be in the middle of a conversation with someone whose cell phone rings, and he or she stops talking to us in order to answer the call. When this happens, we feel as if we don't have the person's attention; as if what we were saying was insignificant; that we're not very important to that person.

In the same way, when we're easily distracted by ringing phones, buzzing doorbells, or whining dogs, we're communicating to the Lord that we're not really paying attention to Him. Our time with Him needs to be focused, directed, and uninterrupted.

Principle #4: Let the Holy Spirit Direct Your Body and Soul

Habits are hard to form, but they're very easy to break. I heard someone say once that it takes three weeks to form a habit. I don't know whether that's true, but I do know from experience that it takes only a single day to break a good habit. My point is that while we can be devoted to developing the habit of seeking God's presence, we must be aware that this is one habit the enemy does not want us to form. He will try all sorts of tricks to make us break the habit of spending meaningful time alone with God each day.

This brings me to the fourth principle. There will be days when we don't feel like entering into God's presence to be alone with Him. Count on it. When we're stressed, overtired, too busy, really upset, or just plain out of sorts, spending time with the Lord and worshipping Him may be the very last thing we feel like doing. But this is actually when we most need to be with Him.

On days like this, we can't base our decision of whether to spend an intimate quiet time with the Lord on our "soulish" feelings. We must allow the Holy Spirit, through our spirit, to direct our body and soul, telling them that we will spend time in His presence, regardless of whether we feel like it or not!

Principle #5: Spend "Meaning-full" Time with the Lord

If we desire intimacy with someone, we must be willing to invest meaningful time into the relationship. This is true, whether it's a relationship between a husband and a wife, a parent and a child, or two friends, and it's especially true if we want an intimate relationship with God.

For time spent with God to be meaningful, it must be "full of meaning" for both Him and me. It must be valuable. It must cost me something. Like King David, we shouldn't offer God what cost us nothing. (See 1 Chronicles 21:24.) If the time we spend with the Lord isn't meaningful to us, we can't expect it to be meaningful to Him.

Spending meaningful time in God's presence is a choice. It's a decision. It's a response to His invitation as He calls you to *"come away"* and be alone with Him.

(See Song of Solomon 2:10 NKJV.) As you respond to the promptings of His Holy Spirit, your time alone with Him will be "meaning-full."

Principle #6: Begin at the Bronze Altar but End Up in the Holy of Holies

Throughout this book, I've reminded you of the five words the Lord spoke to my spirit in that hotel coffee shop many years ago:

Repent. Praise. Worship. Offering. Sacrifice.

Although I was unaware that morning of the journey on which I was about to embark, God has faithfully led me on the pathway leading to His presence by revealing the pictures, patterns, and mysteries of Moses' tabernacle and Solomon's temple. Through the years, He has deepened my knowledge and understanding of how these five words directly relate to what happens in the outer court, the inner court, and the Holy of Holies.

But He also has revealed something else to me.

Every day, when I *"come away"* to spend some quiet time with Him, these five words are themselves the pathway leading me into His presence! Keep in mind that this isn't a formula for intimacy with God; it's simply the pattern He's given us to follow.

I begin with repenting for my daily sins. I gratefully praise Him for what He has done, is doing, and will do in my life and in the lives of my loved ones. In humility and awe, I worship Him for who He is. I offer myself to Him with abandon, and I trustingly give myself to Him as a living sacrifice.

We can't do this by ourselves. We need God's help to repent. Without His grace, our flesh doesn't want to praise and worship Him. Without His strength, we'll be too selfish to offer ourselves to Him with abandon and too afraid to die daily as a living sacrifice to Him.

However, with God's help, grace, and strength, we are able to gladly and willingly lay before Him all of our time, talent, and treasure—all of *ourselves*—for the sake of experiencing an intimate relationship with Him and for the joy of having His presence in our life.

In His Presence

Contrary to what we may have learned in Sunday school, we can't become intimate with the Lord simply by praying and reading His Word. All we end up with is head knowledge. You may win Bible trivia contests with all you know "about" Him. But it's possible to know all about Him, only to one day discover you don't really "know" Him. And we get to know Him and experience genuine intimacy with Him only by spending time in His presence.

My friend, when we come before God cleansed from our sin, when we come before Him with our praises, when we come before Him in worship, when we come before Him as an offering, and when we come before Him as living sacrifices, something wonderful happens. God's presence comes! His love surrounds us! His glory covers us! His peace envelops us! And our spirit is one with His in intimacy.

The wonderful thing about God's presence is that anything—*anything*—can happen in our intimate times with Him. We can be...

+ forgiven!

+ reconciled!

+ healed!

+ freed!

+ restored!

+ transformed!

When we're with Him, there is nothing else we need. His love is all-sufficient, and it's His love that is calling us to press in to a deeper, more intimate relationship with Him.

There's a simple worship song I appreciate so much that describes His amazing love for us...a love that draws us to passionately pursue the pathway leading to His presence. It's called "Oh How He Loves You and Me."

> Oh how He loves you and me,
> Oh how He loves you and me;
> He gave His life, what more could He give?
> Oh how He loves you,
> Oh how He loves me,

Oh how He loves you and me.
Jesus to Calvary did go,
His love for mankind to show;
What He did there brought hope from despair
Oh how He loves you,
Oh how He loves me,
Oh how He loves you and me.

—Kurt Kaiser, 1975

My friend, what Paul so clearly told the Christians living in Rome thousands of years ago is still true for us today:

Who will separate us from the love of Christ? Will tribulation, or distress, or persecution, or famine, or nakedness, or peril, or sword?...But in all these things we overwhelmingly conquer through Him who loved us. For I am convinced that neither death, nor life, nor angels, nor principalities, nor things present, nor things to come, nor powers, nor height, nor depth, nor any other created thing, will be able to separate us from the love of God, which is in Christ Jesus our Lord. (Romans 8:35, 37–39)

My Prayer for You

I'd like to encourage you today in your journey toward intimacy with the Lord. Let me pray for you now.

Lord God, thank You so much for the blood of Your Son that covers us. Thank You that because of His death on the cross, we can boldly approach Your throne of grace in time of need. In Jesus' name, we repent of those things we've done that have not glorified You, and we repent of those things we should have done out of obedience to You but failed to do.

God, we praise You for who You are and what You are doing in our lives. Thank You that Your love will not let us go. Thank You that You have redeemed us and are leading us on the pathway to Your presence.

We worship You because You are God and You are good. You are faithful and true. There is no other god beside You. You alone are worthy to receive all glory and honor and power and praise. Hallelujah!

Lord God, we give ourselves to You as an offering. We lay before You our time, our talent, and our treasure. We hold nothing back. Like King David, we say that everything in the heavens and earth is Yours, O Lord, and this is Your kingdom. All that we have and all that we are, are Yours.

We offer ourselves to You as a living sacrifice, and we choose to die daily, that You might live through us.

God, let this be a day of new beginnings for my friend who is praying this prayer with me right now. May today be a turning point in his or her relationship with You. In the name of Jesus, release the blessing of a one hundredfold relationship with You. Release a new hunger and a new passion for Your presence.

In Jesus' name, make Your child forever discontent to remain in the outer court and even the inner court. By Your grace, help him or her to boldly come into the Holy of Holies. Lord, let Your precious one dwell there, live there, and camp there in Your presence before Your altar, in worship of You. May Your child's life be a sweet-smelling fragrance before You.

Thank You, God, that according to Your Word, You will meet with us and speak with us in this holy place. We bless You, God, in Jesus' name. Amen.

So Press In!

My friend, there's one last thought I want to share with you.

There is a process to developing intimacy with the Lord. It's one thing to know Him as Savior and to experience the joy of salvation in the thirtyfold outer court. But it's a different thing altogether to press into a deeper, more intimate relationship with Him found in the one hundredfold relationship of the Holy of Holies. And it's this type of relationship that He desires to have with us.

In any relationship, intimacy doesn't happen overnight. It takes time to create an intimate relationship with the Lord. Know that God's love is drawing you in and that He is cheering you on. Be patient with yourself in the process, knowing that He is patiently waiting for you.

The cry of Paul's heart was that he would *"know Him and the power of His resurrection"* (Philippians 3:10). Today, may this be the cry of your heart, as well. May God give you the hunger, courage, and faith to respond to His love and press into the Holy of Holies. May you passionately pursue the pathway leading to His presence and abide there with Him forever.

Press in!

ABOUT THE AUTHOR

As chairman and CEO of Inspiration Ministries in Indian Land, South Carolina, David Cerullo is dedicated to impacting people for Christ worldwide through media. He is a unique combination of Christian minister and corporate businessman. The son of international evangelist Morris Cerullo, David took a less traditional approach to ministry, graduating from Oral Roberts University with a degree in business administration and management. Inspiration TV currently reaches more than 150 nations with the gospel of Jesus Christ. David and his wife, Barbara, host a daily international television outreach program, *Inspiration Today!* For more information, visit **inspiration.org**.